I0023446

Alexander Thom

Return of judicial rents fixed by Sub-Commissioners and Civil Bill Courts

notified to Irish Land Commission

Alexander Thom

Return of judicial rents fixed by Sub-Commissioners and Civil Bill Courts
notified to Irish Land Commission

ISBN/EAN: 9783742800220

Manufactured in Europe, USA, Canada, Australia, Japa

Cover: Foto ©Thomas Meinert / pixelio.de

Manufactured and distributed by brebook publishing software
(www.brebook.com)

Alexander Thom

Return of judicial rents fixed by Sub-Commissioners and Civil Bill Courts

Irish Land Commission.

The Land Law (Ireland) Act, 1881, 44 & 45 Victoria, ch. 49

The Land Law (Ireland) Act, 1887, 50 & 51 Victoria, ch. 33.

RETURN

ACCORDING TO PROVINCES AND COUNTIES

OF

JUDICIAL RENTS

FIXED BY

CHIEF COMMISSION,

SUB-COMMISSIONS,

AND

CIVIL BILL COURTS,

AS NOTIFIED TO THE IRISH LAND COMMISSION DURING THE MONTH OF

JUNE, 1891,

SPECIFYING DATES AND AMOUNTS RESPECTIVELY OF THE LAST INCREASES
OF RENT WHERE ASCERTAINED;

ALSO

RENTS FIXED UPON THE REPORTS OF VALUERS APPOINTED BY THE IRISH LAND
COMMISSION ON THE JOINT APPLICATIONS OF LANDLORDS AND TENANTS.

Presented to both Houses of Parliament by Command of Her Majesty.

DUBLIN:

PRINTED FOR HER MAJESTY'S STATIONERY OFFICE

BY

ALEXANDER THOM & CO. (LIMITED),

And to be purchased, either directly or through any Bookseller, from
HODGES, FIGGIS, and Co., 104, Grafton-street, Dublin; or
EYRE and SPOTTISWOODE, East Harding-street, Fleet-street, E.C.; or
JOHN MENZIES and Co., 12, Hanover-street, Edinburgh, and 90, West Nile-street, Glasgow.

INDEX.

SUMMARIES FOR JUNE, 1891.

Summary showing, according to Provinces and Counties, the Number of Cases in which Judicial Rents have been Fixed by Chief Commission and Sub-Commissions, under the Land Law (Ireland) Act, 1881, during the Month of June, 1891; and the Acreage, Tenement Valuations, Former Rents, and Judicial Rents of the Holdings.

Provinces and County.	Number of Cases in which Judicial Rents have been Fixed	Acreage.			Tenement Valuation.			Former Rent.			Judicial Rent.		
		Statute Acres.			£	s.	d.	£	s.	d.	£	s.	d.
		A.	R.	P.									
ULSTER—													
Antrim,	1	17	0	8	16	0	0	17	5	0	15	0	0
Armagh,	34	531	2	30	278	16	1	215	10	8	238	16	8
Cavan,	48	1,096	5	17	627	7	0	491	9	8	454	19	0
Monaghan,	52	765	0	36	517	10	0	670	13	6	483	19	0
Tyrone,	17	761	1	16	374	0	0	416	0	0	579	1	0
Totals,	156	8,009	0	18	1,831	13	3	1,876	16	8	1,555	2	6
LEINSTER—													
Carlow,	3	137	0	6	33	10	0	55	15	0	29	0	6
Dublin,	4	611	1	36	808	5	0	623	10	6	631	15	0
Kildare,	55	1,331	1	19	1,039	10	0	1,542	6	3	1,343	1	4
Kilkenny,	20	399	0	14	534	0	0	534	5	11	471	5	0
King's,	8	301	1	39	75	6	0	54	17	2	46	0	8
Longford,	8	39	1	13	21	18	0	31	14	6	15	5	8
Louth,	10	816	1	16	312	5	0	336	15	8	239	15	0
Meath,	17	1,130	0	3	980	15	0	1,211	14	3	956	15	0
Queen's,	7	196	3	36	130	10	0	180	11	10	134	0	6
Westmeath,	61	2,148	3	39	1,227	15	0	1,615	8	4	1,017	10	3
Wexford,	24	1,035	3	6	971	15	0	657	11	11	616	14	10
Wicklow,	55	3:1	1	16	606	5	0	779	6	5	547	11	10
Totals,	254	8,877	5	17	5,761	7	0	7,508	9	7	6,137	16	3
CONNAUGHT—													
Galway,	150	4,133	3	33	1,499	11	0	2,051	4	4	1,406	5	8
Leitrim,	15	291	2	13	123	1	0	163	0	9	119	4	10
Mayo,	47	1,070	3	6	275	1	6	337	2	7	263	11	10
Roscommon,	95	1,116	0	33	434	10	5	523	0	5	373	2	6
Sligo,	63	1,381	0	34	899	12	0	1,006	14	6	776	1	3
Totals,	378	8,593	0	31	3,231	9	2	4,080	4	5	3,032	15	3
MUNSTER—													
Clare,	6	150	1	30	109	15	0	134	10	9	99	0	8
Cork,	85	5,795	0	4	1,347	5	0	1,590	14	9	1,373	13	0
Limerick,	9	339	1	30	197	5	0	217	6	8	160	5	0
Tipperary,	72	1,176	1	33	1,364	16	0	1,718	17	3½	1,590	13	5
Waterford,	5	249	0	13	103	16	0	119	18	0	90	10	0
Totals,	174	7,014	1	94	3,082	1	0	4,078	1	6½	3,109	1	6

IRELAND.

ULSTER,	156	8,009	0	18	1,831	13	3	1,876	16	8	1,555	2	6
LEINSTER,	254	8,877	5	17	5,761	7	0	7,508	9	7	6,137	16	3
CONNAUGHT,	378	8,593	0	31	3,231	9	2	4,080	4	5	3,032	15	4
MUNSTER,	174	7,014	1	94	3,082	1	0	4,078	1	6½	3,109	1	4
Totals,	968	33,508	3	13	13,866	9	4	17,739	13	11½	13,897	15	6

Note.—For Values' Duties, see pp. 62–64.

CIVIL BILL COURTS.

SUMMARY FOR JUNE, 1891.

Cases in which Judicial Rents have been fixed by Civil Bill Courts under the Land Law (Ireland) Act, 1881, and notified to the Irish Land Commission during the Month of June, 1891.

Province and County.	Number of Cases in which Judicial Rents have been fixed.	Acreage.	Standard Valuation.	Former Rent.	Judicial Rent.
		Statute Acres. A. R. P.	£ s. d.	£ s. d.	£ s. d.
ULSTER—					
Armagh,	7	87 1 34	61 0 0	73 14 1	58 4 5
Cavan,	24	408 3 4	232 15 0	263 4 11½	203 9 5
Totals,	31	496 0 38	293 15 0	336 18 0½	261 14 0
LEINSTER—					
Kildare,	5	138 3 21	88 15 0	95 4 2	73 7 0
Meath,	1	186 1 4	150 0 0	250 0 0	156 0 0
Westmeath,	1	36 0 31	13 0 0	14 0 0	12 0 0
Totals,	7	322 1 16	232 10 0	330 4 3	231 7 0
CONNAUGHT—					
Mayo,	3	16 0 10	8 5 0	14 18 3½	10 0 0
MUNSTER—					
Cork,	17	713 2 51	330 10 0	321 17 0	218 10 0
Kerry,	29	1,108 0 23	316 13 0	464 0 0	335 17 0
Totals,	46	1,822 3 4	646 8 0	843 17 0	604 7 0

IRELAND.

ULSTER,	31	528 0 36	299 15 0	336 18 0½	261 14 0
LEINSTER,	7	822 1 16	232 15 0	809 4 3	221 7 0
CONNAUGHT,	3	16 0 10	8 5 0	14 18 3½	10 0 0
MUNSTER,	46	1,823 3 4	646 8 0	843 17 0	604 7 0
Totals,	86	2,632 1 38	1,187 8 0	1,504 19 1	1,097 8 0

Printed image donated by the University of Southampton Library Digitisation Unit

LEASEHOLDERS.

SUMMARY FOR JUNE, 1891.

Summary showing, according to Provinces and Counties, the number of Cases in which Judicial Rents have been fixed by Chief Commission and Sub-Commissions, under the Land Law (Ireland) Act, 1887, during the Month of June, 1891, and also the Acreage, Tenement Valuations, Former Rents, and Judicial Rents of the Holdings.

Provinces and County.	Number of Cases in which Judicial Rents have been fixed.	Acreage.			Tenement Valuation.			Former Rent.			Judicial Rent.		
		A.	R.	P.	£	s.	d.	£	s.	d.	£	s.	d.
ULSTER—													
Antrim,	1	9	0	0	---			3	12	1	4	10	0
Armagh,	4	39	1	31	20	0	0	35	7	6½	31	0	0
Cavan,	31	982	3	19	645	3	0	791	19	11	913	0	5
Down,	4	63	2	8	100	0	0	116	4	10	77	4	3
Monaghan,	8	314	3	36	283	13	0	231	19	7	173	10	0
Tyrone,	16	651	3	30	278	5	0	239	1	6	234	1	0
Totals,	57	1,863	1	84	1,174	1	0	1,433	19	8½	1,116	9	8
LEINSTER—													
Carlow,	1	53	3	14	63	0	0	137	0	0	78	0	0
Dublin,	10	573	0	0½	1,066	0	0	1,473	18	8	1,138	6	1
Kildare,	89	6,185	1	16	5,115	6	0	3,639	5	2	3,189	0	5
Kilkenny,	16	979	1	8	698	5	0	808	13	6	845	11	3
King's,	8	1,634	1	17	631	10	0	911	0	11	779	0	0
Louth,	4	427	2	20	533	19	0	410	11	2	843	3	0
Meath,	16	1,301	8	27	1,730	1	0	2,234	16	11	1,730	10	0
Queen's,	8	893	0	13½	895	0	0	2,007	17	8	652	7	10
Westmeath,	16	1,612	3	3	1,576	15	0	1,375	12	0	1,547	0	0
Wexford,	25	1,741	3	30	708	10	0	664	13	10	661	18	8
Wicklow,	13	2,408	0	1	1,743	13	0	1,083	14	6	1,633	16	0
Totals,	165	16,104	0	9½	19,054	4	0	15,364	14	5	12,433	16	10
CONNAUGHT—													
Galway,	36	4,256	0	19	1,378	14	0	1,359	19	3	1,290	9	4
Leitrim,	6	349	3	55	119	0	0	131	3	6	116	4	0
Mayo,	3	434	2	11	197	0	0	170	0	4	169	10	0
Roscommon,	3	354	1	14	367	10	0	731	6	6	183	17	6
Sligo,	8	843	3	21	190	13	0	223	10	6	183	17	6
Totals,	63	5,340	2	30	1,870	17	0	3,711	1	9	1,895	7	0
MUNSTER—													
Clare,	11	698	1	33	240	3	0	793	3	11	311	10	0
Cork,	37	4,598	8	38	3,775	1	0	3,733	2	9	2,703	11	4
Limerick,	43	7,827	0	19	1,965	9	0	3,441	17	6	2,143	16	0
Tipperary,	46	4,434	0	51½	1,718	18	0	3,305	17	9	1,778	3	3
Waterford,	33	3,223	3	52	1,050	4	0	1,983	18	9	1,394	16	0
Totals,	733	15,025	8	12½	7,765	9	0	11,243	14	6	8,131	18	6

IRELAND.

CIVIL BILL COURTS.

LEASEHOLDERS.

SUMMARY FOR JUNE, 1891.

Cases in which Judicial Rents have been fixed by Civil Bill Courts, under the Land Law (Ireland) Act, 1887, and notified to the Irish Land Commission during the Month of June, 1891.

Province and County	Number of Cases in which Judicial Rents have been fixed	Acreage	Previous Valuation	Former Rent	Judicial Rent
		Statute Acres.			
		a. r. p.	£ s. d.	£ s. d.	£ s. d.
ULSTER—					
Armagh, —	1	32 0 19	—	41 15 0	50 0 0
Cavan, —	5	159 2 33	114 0 0	140 14 5	100 18 0
Totals, ...	6	191 3 13	114 0 0	153 9 5	130 18 0
LEINSTER—					
Dublin, —	1	11 0 33	72 0 0	29 1 0	51 15 10
Kildare, —	2	146 0 29	110 5 0	148 0 0	145 0 0
Meath, —	3	87 3 30	53 0 0	157 0 0	57 0 0
Totals, ...	5	245 0 31	196 5 0	325 5 5	775 15 10
MUNSTER—					
Kerry, ...	27	1,490 3 35	879 1 0	641 15 10	435 1 9

IRELAND.

ULSTER, —	6	191 3 13	114 0 0	153 9 5	130 18 0
LEINSTER, ...	5	245 0 31	196 5 0	325 5 6	225 15 10
MUNSTER, ...	27	1,490 3 35	879 1 0	641 15 10	435 1 9
TOTALS, ...	38	1,927 8 25	689 6 0	1,125 10 9	811 15 7

Names of Assistant Constabulars by whom Case was Settled.	No.	Name of Tenant.	Name of Landlord.	Townland.
HEAD CONSTABLE.	6187	George A. Gray, ...	Julia M. Lyons, ...	... Glenngary, ...

Assistant Constabulars—				
E. Gaum (Legal),	8420	Samuel G. Gawden, Ltd. Admrs. of Annie Gawden.	Earl of Kilmorey, ...	Attameolgh, ...
T. Smyth,	8421	Do, ...	do.	do.
J. H. McConnell.	8422	Do, ...	do.	do.
	8433	Anna Lawson, ...	Captain R. R. McDonough Bond,	Mountshill, ...
	8474	Do, ...	do.	do.
	6475	Bernard Murphy & exor. Exors. of Patrick Murphy and another.	G. F. C. Henry & others, Trustees of Thomas G. Henry.	Scaliu, ...
	8476	Sarah Irwin, ...	Major William J. Hall,	Gosaik, ...
	8477	Fanny Irwin, ...	do.	Cloghancusey and another.
	8478	Daniel Sherdin, Reps. of Bernard Sherdin.	G. H. J. Alexander, ...	Lymalessoro, ...
	8479	Susan Hardy, ...	Rev. J. White Reid,	Ballorilee, ...
	8450	William Henlip, ...	Earl of Kilmorey, ...	Drumdelice, ...
	8451	Do, ...	do.	Clogbamidete, ...
	8452	Do, ...	do.	Drumslane, ...
	8453	Edward McShane, ...	Granville H. Alexander, ...	Tiffeeny, ...
	8454	Hugh McCoy, ...	John McCullough,	Ghautropmeash, ...
	8415	Christy Murphy, ...	do.	Gannally, ...
	8436	Catherine Irvine, Rep. of John Irvine.	John McCullough and another,	do.
	8437	Thomas O'Hare, ...	do.	do.
	8438	Owen Murphy, ...	do.	do.
	8439	Thomas McGlim, Rep. of	do.	do.

ULSTER.

ANTRIM.

Amount of Holding.	Poor Law Valuation.	Former Rent.	Judicial Rent.	Observations.
A. R. P.	£ s. d.	£ s. d.	£ s. d.	
17 0 5	16 0 0	17 5 0	13 0 0	The rent in this case … ognment of the ye… sitting of the Court …

ARMAGH.

6 5 0	5 5 0	4 1 6	4 4 6
4 5 9	6 15 0	3 10 10	3 10 10
6 1 01	6 5 0	5 17 0	5 5 0
20 0 5	14 0 0	15 11 0	11 5 0
5 1 10	unascertained	5 5 10	5 5 10
5 3 57	6 15 0	4 17 0	6 7 6
35 3 16	38 10 0	71 0 0	15 5 0
19 0 16	91 0 0	16 10 0	14 10 0
11 3 10	6 5 0	5 16 10	5 5 0
6 1 13	5 0 3	4 0 0	6 10 0
3 5 15	5 15 0	4 0 10	5 5 0
1 5 6	6 0 0	3 6 8	5 0 0
1 5 6	unascertained	5 5 0	7 5 0
14 1 50	30 0 0	30 5 0	19 0 0
5 5 16	unascertained	1 5 6	1 0 0
9 1 13	5 10 0	5 6 5	4 5 0
4 1 0	1 15 0	5 0 0	1 0 0
1 5 50	—	1 11 5	1 11 5
10 5 0	5 5 0	5 15 7	5 10 0
57 1 50	6 15 0	50 0 0	15 0 0

COUNTY OF

Name of Assistant Commissioner by whom Case was Certified.	No.	Name of Tenant.	Name of Landlord.	Townland.
Assistant Commissioners— E. Carew (Legal) T. Sayer. J. H. McConnell.	5490	Hugh McEvoy,	George Atkinson,	Lower Fathom,
	5491	Robert McGrath,	Cecilia E. Copp and anor., Executors of Francis R. Copp, a banaffes.	Lisadyhag,
	5492	Edmund McKeown,	George Patton,	Drumilly,
	5493	Patrick Burns,	Reps. of Trevor A. Hanna,	Carrick,
	5494	Elizabeth Willis,	Lord Castlingford,	Roughlahera,
	5495	Thomas Ogishby,	do.	do.
	5496	Lambert Cardwell,	Major F. E. Hall,	Derrymore,
	5497	Ellen McParland,	Robert E. Gleerig,	Annaclonghaulin,
	5498	James Mann, Rep. of Mathew Mann.	Captain L. Thompson,	Derrimond,
	5499	Do.	do.	do.
	5500	James Kealy,	do.	do.
	5501	Patrick Klaks, junior,	Captain E.H. McGeough Bagot,	Kinentriel,
	5502	Bridget Lambe, Ltd. Admrs. of Bryan Lambe (Fair).	do.	do.
	5503	Bryan McArdle,	do.	do.
				Total,

COUNTY OF

Assistant Commissioners— J. H. Ryan (Legal). G. N. Campbell. G. M. Harvey.	3704	Bridget McCabe,	Marquis of Headfort,	Virginia,
	3705	Do.	do.	do.
	3706	Ellen Whitely,	do.	Carrick,
	3707	Michael Maginghlin,	do.	Eighter,
	5708	Patrick Carroll,	do.	do.
	5709	Thomas Parrelly,	do.	Crossadds,
	3710	Mary Maughan,	do.	Eighter,
	3711	Thomas Uihney,	do.	Charick,
	3712	Catherine Reilly,	do.	Enagh,
	3713	Richard Carroll,	do.	Edenburt,
	3714	Do.	do.	do.
	3715	William Prath,	Marcus Beresford and others, Reps. of J. Beresford.	Gallon,

ARMAGH—*continued*.

Extent of Holding. Statute.	Poor Law Valuation.	Former Rent.	Judicial Rent.	Observations.
a. r. p.	£ s. d.	£ s. d.	£ s. d.	
2 2 0	3 15 0	4 13 0	8 0 0	By consent.
16 1 13	13 10 0	12 0 0	10 13 0	
6 0 13	6 10 0	7 9 6	7 9 6	
6 0 0	4 6 0	3 3 10	9 2 10	
6 1 10	4 10 0	6 6 0	6 6 6	
14 1 20	10 6 0	7 6 6	7 6 0	
4 3 13	unascertained,	6 9 3	6 0 0	
16 1 20	7 6 6	6 12 6	6 16 0	do.
6 0 0	18 6 6	9 4 6	7 10 0	
13 1 30	16 0 0	10 7 6	9 10 0	
40 0 0	44 6 0	36 0 0	29 0 0	
11 3 26	6 10 0	6 13 0	6 11 0	
9 1 30	6 19 0	6 3 0	6 16 0	
6 3 23	4 6 0	4 3 6	6 9 6	
101 3 20	279 15 2	776 10 6	226 16 6	

CAVAN.

34 3 0	16 6 6	16 16 2	16 10 0	
36 3 6	30 0 0	34 10 6	26 6 0	
63 6 16	11 10 6	12 16 10	11 0 0	
11 3 10	6 10 6	6 2 6	6 6 0	
30 0 11	31 6 0	33 9 6	30 0 0	
34 1 6	26 6 6	29 17 6	31 0 0	
11 1 13	6 3 6	7 3 0	6 0 0	
40 3 6	26 0 6	30 7 0	31 0 0	
43 0 36	19 16 0	22 7 0	17 0 0	
16 1 10	unascertained,	11 19 6	9 16 0	
6 3 0	do.	7 17 0	6 0 0	
44 0 22	33 16 0	23 3 6	23 0 0	

Name of Assistant Commissioners by whom Case was decided.	No.	Name of Tenant.	Name of Landlord.
Assistant Commissioners—			
W. F. BAILEY (Legal). Q. J. CALLWELL. Q. M. HARVEY.	3716	Owen Lynch,	Oliver S. Segrave,
	3717	Hugh Clarke,	do.
	3718	John Walsh,	do.
	3719	Terence Brady,	Lord Charles Beresford
	3720	Owen Lynch,	Robert Stacey,
	3721	Philip Farrelly,	Ellen Brady,
	3722	Francis Harrison,	Robert Stacey,
	3723	Ross McCabe,	do.
	3724	Joseph Cullen,	do.
	3725	Anne Finnegan, Admx. of Patrick Finnegan,	do.
	3726	John Cullen,	do.
	3727	Ross McCabe,	Major Caning,
	3728	John Evans,	Lord Farnham,
	3729	Philip Connell,	Marquis of Headfort,
	3730	Samuel Bowrt,	Sarah A. Dinham,
	3731	James Farrell,	O. D. Fox,
	3732	Anne Reilly,	Allan Nesbitt,
	3733	Mary Keegan,	do.
	3734	Margaret Cullen, Admx. of Thomas Cullen,	do.
	3735	Thomas McManus,	do.
	3736	James Brady,	Robert Stacey,
	3737	Anne M. Mathews,	Arthur Rothwell,
	3738	John Brady,	James Erskine,
	3739	Obadiah H. Williamson,	Lady Lisgar,

CAVAN—*continued.*

Extent of Holding. Roods.	Poor Law Valuation.	Former Rent.	Judicial Rent.	Observations.

COUNTY OF

Name of Assistant Commissioners by whom Cases were decided.	No.	Name of Tenant.	Name of Landlord.	Townland.
Assistant Commissioners:—				
W. F. Bailey (Legal). G. N. Caldwell. G. M. Harvey.	8749	David Nelson, ...	Samuel A. Adams, —	Derry, —
	3750	Mathew Donnelly, ...	Rev. R. A. Hall, —	Raghmore, —
	3751	Do. ...	do. ...	do. —
	8752	James Nulty, ...	Peter Farrelly, —	Rahoya, —
				Total, —

COUNTY OF

Assistant Commissioners:—				
F. Greer (Legal). T. Davidson. J. Pattinson.	3268	Owen Bermingham, ...	H. W. G. Crofton, ...	Craigabawn, ...
	3269	John Mitchell, ...	H. F. McMath, —	Kiltrea, ...
	8270	Michael Brady, ...	H. J. McMath, —	Tincrill, ...
	8271	Mary Connolly, ...	Mrs. Sarah McMath, ...	Tullynabury, ...
	8272	Edward Markey, ...	Jane Hamill and others, ...	Slit, ...
	8273	Catharine Tomney, ...	Vincent Templeton, —	Croaghan, ...
	8274	Francis Morgan, ...	do. —	do. ...
	8275	Catharine Carr, Ltd. Admin. of Anne Carr.	do. —	Killyreaghan, ...
	8276	Francis Dorley, Rep. of Alice McHugh.	do. —	Usher, ...
	8277	Nancy McQuaid, ...	do. ...	Kinniego, ...
	8278	James McKee, ...	do. ...	Conaghty, ...
	8279	Hugh McKee, ...	do. ...	do. ...
	8280	Do. ...	do. —	do. ...
	8281	Patrick Fealy, ...	Richard E. Fitzherbert, ...	Keeloff, ...
	8282	George Geoghegan, ...	do. ...	Drumquilford, —
	8283	Robert Burgess, ...	do. —	do. ...
	8284	John Moffat, ...	do. ...	Reehill, ...
	8285	Bridget Duffy, Ltd. Admin. of Mary Duffy.	do. ...	do. ...
	8286	Mary Sheridan, ...	do. ...	Slough, ...
	8287	Michael Keenan, Limtd. ...	do. ...	do. ...

CAVAN—continued.

Extent of Holdings. Roods.	Poor Law Valuation.	Present Rent.	Judicial Rent.	Observations.
A. R. P.	£ s. d.	£ s. d.	£ s. d.	
43 2 2	17 15 0	18 2 0	21 10 0	
19 3 25	12 5 0	12 8 0	8 10 0	
15 1 20	10 10 0	10 10 0	8 10 0	
2 2 20	1 10 0	1 13 4	1 0 0	
1,000 2 17	827 7 0	847 9 3	555 10 0	

MONAGHAN.

7 1 8	8 13 0	3 8 0	2 0 0	
4 3 20	3 15 0	5 5 0	4 10 0	
19 0 15	13 0 0	14 17 8	11 10 0	
11 8 20	7 10 0	9 4 8	7 5 0	
15 0 5	10 5 0	10 7 5	8 0 0	
24 1 30	17 0 0	17 18 9	15 5 0	
17 3 25	7 0 0	8 17 9	6 0 0	
8 3 10	7 0 0	7 4 0	5 13 0	
19 8 10	8 15 0	9 10 0	7 8 0	
8 0 3	5 15 0	7 4 0	8 15 8	
15 1 30	8 10 0	5 8 0	7 0 0	
20 3 3	16 15 0	16 11 5	15 10 0	
19 0 5	5 10 0	5 15 0	5 15 0	
11 1 20	8 15 0	9 0 9	7 10 0	
16 1 20	13 10 0	13 4 9	9 5 0	
24 1 0	20 0 0	17 8 0	15 0 0	
8 3 20	6 15 0	5 19 0	5 0 0	
4 3 10	3 13 0	8 19 0	3 0 8	
19 3 5	11 8 0	10 11 0	8 9 0	
10 3 15	7 5 0	5 14 0	6 15 0	
16 0 15	11 5 0	10 6 0	8 10 0	
21 8 15	13 0 0	11 9 0	13 10 0	
11 0 25	7 8 0	7 2 0	8 0 0	
15 5 35	8 15 0	9 11 0	8 0 0	
10 3 0	6 10 0	5 5 0	5 8 0	

Name of Assistant Commissioners by whom Cases were decided.	No.	Name of Tenant.	Name of Landlord.
Assistant Commissioners—			
R. Green (Legal). T. Davidson. J. Patterson.	5233	Elizabeth Reilly, Ltd. Admin. of Edward Reilly.	Richard H. Robertson.
	5234	James Swinney,	do.	—
	5235	Do.	do.	—
	5236	John Connolly,	do.	—
	5237	Peter McCabe,	do.	—
	5238	Anne Connolly,	do.	—
	5239	James Marron,	do.	—
	5240	James Swinney,	do.	—
	5241	Do.	do.	—
	5242	Patrick McMahon,	do.	—
	5243	John Daly,	do.	—
	5244	Margaret Daly,	do.	—
	5245	Michael Daly,	do.	—
	5246	Bad Connolly,	do.	—
	5247	Michael Marron, Rep. of Peter Marron.	do.	—
	5248	Hugh Connolly,	do.	—
	5249	James Connolly,	do.	—
	5250	Patrick Connolly,	do.	—
	5251	Do.	do.	—
	5252	Hugh McCabe,	do.	—
	5253	Owen Burns,	do.	—
	5254	Philip Connolly,	do.	—
	5255	Peter Lynch,	do.	—
	5256	Michael Connolly, Ltd. Admr. of Francis Connolly.	do.	—
	5257	William Daly,	do.	—
W. F. Bailey (Legal). T. Davidson. J. Patterson.	5258	Bridget Casey,	Doctor Hamilton,	
	5259	Denis Ward,	Mrs. Letitia Bewshaw street.	
	5260	Joseph Bailey,	William Teynham,	
	5261	Francis Parkin,	do.	—
	5262	James McEnEntegy,	do.	—

MONAGHAN—continued

Extent of Holdings	Poor Law Valuation.	Former Rent.	Judicial Rent.	Observations.	Value of Tenancy.
A. R. P.	£ s. d.	£ s. d.	£ s. d.		£ s. d.
85 0 37	15 0 0	16 13 0	14 0 0		
14 3 03	mountain land.	11 8 0	8 10 0		
4 2 4	do.	8 13 0	8 15 0		
10 3 50	8 0 0	7 15 0	6 12 0		
15 1 5	13 10 0	12 0 0	10 5 0		
8 3 55	6 6 0	7 1 0	5 15 0		
57 1 90	18 0 0	22 1 0	17 10 0		
91 3 2	mountain land.	14 8 0	13 0 0		
6 3 84	do.	5 0 0	3 15 0		
15 1 0	11 0 0	11 18 0	8 5 0		
11 0 20	8 15 0	11 8 4	7 15 0		
22 3 30	17 0 0	17 5 0	14 10 0		
26 3 84	18 5 0	20 18 0	16 10 0		
7 3 15	6 0 0	5 3 6	4 12 0		
7 3 32	5 3 0	5 8 0	6 15 0		
10 0 5	8 5 0	8 8 0	7 8 8		
15 3 15	10 15 0	11 13 0	9 8 0		
34 2 15	33 10 0	19 4 0	16 10 0		
5 3 55	6 15 0	5 0 0	4 5 0		
10 8 20	8 5 0	8 4 0	5 10 0		
6 3 5	8 10 0	9 15 0	8 8 0		
17 8 55	8 8 0	8 13 0	7 10 0		
8 3 3	7 0 0	7 5 0	8 10 0		
11 1 10	11 0 0	8 10 0	7 8 0		
58 3 8	18 5 0	20 8 0	18 0 0		
16 3 11	13 0 0	11 1 4	8 0 8		
14 5 0	11 10 0	14 3 8	8 10 0		
15 0 30	15 0 0	15 5 8	8 0 0		
8 0 35	8 0 0	8 15 8	5 0 0		
5 1 35	7 5 0	5 18 6	8 0 8		
786 0 55	817 10 0	870 15 6	445 13 0		

Names of Assistant Commissioners by whom Cases were decided.	No.	Name of Tenant.	Name of Landlord.	Townland.
Assistant Commissioners— E. Green (Legal). J. Ottiwell. W. G. Stee.	7657	Margaret A. Wilson, —	S. R. Hamilton and others, Trustees of William Todd.	Mountjoy Forest, East, —
	7658	Thomas J. McAllister,..	Earl of Belmore, ...	Beaghmore, —
	7659	John Orr, — —	do. — —	Rew, —
	7660	George Graham, —	do. .. —	Dougary, —
	7651	Allen McKenna, Limited Admix. of Patrick McKenna.	Amy H. Emles, a minor, by Dr. Thomas Dervan and others, her Guardians.	Scraggs, —
	7652	Joseph Callivan, ..-	do. ... —	Lisnacloon, —
	7653	Samuel Craignafin, —	do.	Scotin, —
	7654	James Gormley, senior, —	Earl of Castlestuart, —	Garaghmore, —
	7655	John Loughran, —	do. — —	do. —
	7656	Peter Gunn, ,—	do. — ..	do. —
	7657	Frazale Gormley, —	do. — —	do. —
	7643	Bernard Doherty, —	do. — —	Carnavern, —
	7649	Do., —	do. — ..	do. —
	7670	Joseph Anderson and another.	Sir John M. Stewart, Bart.,	Aldrumaned, —
	7671	Arthur McCrory, —	do. — —	Mullentamey, —
	7572	James McKernan, ...	do. — ..	Thomage, —
	7673	Michael McKernan, —	do.	—
				Total, —

PROVINCE OF

Assistant Commissioners—				
J. H. Read (Legal). A. N. Oritt. J. H. Bayar.	1052	Daniel Blanchfield, —	Earl of Charlton, —	Cantogue, —
	1053	James Ross, .. —	do. ... —	do. —
				Total, —

TABLE OF JUDICIAL RENTS.

TYRONE.

Extent of Holding. Acres.	Poor Law Valuation.	Former Rent.	Judicial Rent.	Observations.
A. R. P.	£ s. d.	£ s. d.	£ s. d.	
105 0 0	109 15 0	100 0 0	101 0 0	
30 0 0	29 5 0	29 10 0	23 0 0	By consent.
37 5 0	54 10 0	53 0 0	34 10 0	
61 1 34	39 15 0	37 18 0	31 0 0	
35 0 0	1 10 0	3 0 0	1 9 0	
10 0 3	5 18 0	6 16 0	5 0 0	
15 0 0	unascertained,	6 3 0	7 0 0	
12 3 0	13 0 0	9 3 0	6 15 0	
30 3 25	15 10 0	13 3 0	10 15 0	
19 3 30	unascertained,	7 15 0	6 3 0	
30 3 30	do.	10 3 0	8 0 0	
23 3 19	12 0 0	9 0 0	7 10 0	
73 1 33	34 10 0	23 8 0	30 10 0	
30 3 15	5 15 0	7 0 0	4 13 0	
40 1 10	4 0 0	5 0 0	3 10 0	
43 3 10	3 10 0	3 3 3	3 10 0	
54 3 33	4 3 0	3 13 3	4 0 0	
705 1 13	394 0 0	415 0 0	339 3 0	

LEINSTER.

CARLOW.

COUNTY OF

Names of Assistant Commissioners by whom Cases were decided.	No.	Name of Tenant.	Name of Landlord.	Townland.
Assistant Commissioners:—				
R. R. Kane (Legal). S. Mowbray. P. Clarke.	423	Thomas Fowler,	John Willis,	Ballyorbin,
	424	James Behan,	John Le Poultre,	Crossykeera and eardson
R. R. Kane (Legal). S. Mowbray. R. Martin.	425	Matthew Chiffes; ministe, in behalf of Patrick Chiffes.	Very Rev. H. Jellett, p.p., and others, Trustees of Margaret's Charity.	Richecoole,
	426	Richard Walsh,	Governors of Saint Patrick's Hospital,	Brown's Fairy,
	427	Mrs. Elizabeth Price,	Trustees of Morgan's Charity Schools,	Newcastle,
	428	James Archbold,	Colonel James R. Burton,	Cannagh,
				Total,

COUNTY OF

Names of Assistant Commissioners:—	No.	Name of Tenant.	Name of Landlord.	Townland.
R. R. Kane (Legal). W. A. Hunt. R. Martin.	773	John Nolan,	Vincent Gough,	Prumplestown,
	774	Maria Maher,	Sarah M. Rice and others,	Taghurane,
	775	Matthew Minch,	Miss Arabella Beard,	Ardroe,
	776	Isabella Sopple,	Caroline Graham and another,	Narraling,
	777	Owen McDonald,	Miss Frances Archbold,	Shanagee,
	778	Thomas Byrne,	Thomas Hambrick, mentioned in name of Algernon Aylmer,	Commonstown,
	779	Daniel Fitzpatrick,	Arthur R. Verschoyle,	Lowtown,
	780	John J. Twamley, named in name of Maria Twamley,	James Clarke and others,	Ballytodan,
	781	William Burke,	Mary Harte,	Commonstown,
	782	Thomas Murphy,	Frederick L. Fitzgerald,	Calverton,
	783	John Mahon,	do.	Pumbrastown,
	784	Andrew Byrne,	do.	do.
	785	Thomas Plowman,	Miss Arabella Beard,	Ardroe,
	786	Michael Murphy,	Thomas Butler,	Ballyrue,
	787	Michael Fitzpatrick,	Miss Arabella Beard,	Ardroe,
	788	Michael Cope,	Frederick L. Fitzgerald,	Ballyroggan,
	789	Patrick Dunne and anor.,	Thomas F. Spencer,	Ballyroggan,
	790	William Mooney,	do.	do.
	791	Michael Byrne,	do.	do.
	792	Do.	do.	Ballykelly,

TABLE OF JUDICIAL RENTS.

Former Rent.			Judicial Rent.			Observations.
£	s.	d.	£	s.	d.	
43	0	0	38	0	0	
14	1	0	19	0	0	
4	13	0	3	15	0	
394	15	6	360	0	0	
54	0	0	45	0	0	
180	0	0	13	0	0	
633	10	6	551	15	0	

14	7	3	13	6	0	
34	0	0	28	10	0	
17	11	6	13	10	0	
43	10	0	38	0	0	
18	14	7	17	0	0	
28	10	0	21	5	0	
60	0	0	60	0	0	
38	16	2	34	0	0	
13	0	0	11	0	0	
70	0	0	58	6	0	
13	0	0	9	10	0	
14	0	0	16	0	0	
13	0	0	22	10	0	
38	0	0	29	0	0	
8	0	0	8	0	0	
70	0	0	60	0	0	
30	0	0	23	10	0	
10	0	0	8	0	0	
23	16	0	20	0	0	
24	0	0	16	0	0	

Names of Assistant Commissioners by whom Cases were Settled.	No.	Name of Tenant	Name of Landlord	Townland.
Assistant Commissioners—				
B. R. Kays (Legal). W. S. Hill. S. Baker.	793	Daniel McDermott, administrator of the late McBuchrick	Thomas E. Spencer,	Ballykelly,
	794	John Wheeler,	Mary Hurn,	Currycahaleen,
	795	John McNally,	John LaTrouche,	Toohogein,
	796	Patrick Gorman,	Major Francis Burnham,	Crookstown,
	797	Patrick Kelly,	Elizabeth Kennedy and others,	Stephaun,
	798	Eliza Murphy,	Thomas E. Spencer,	Ballykelly,
	799	Catherine Hynham,	Mary A. Ford,	Grangemoiling,
	800	Patrick Rourke, contd. in name of Mary Fitzpatrick,	Thomas F. Spencer,	Ballykelly,
	801	Edward Lawler,	Henry Thomas, a minor, by Emma J. Thomas, Mr. Committee.	Meane,
	802	Catherine Hynham,	Sir Anthony C. Weldon, Bart.	Grangemoiling,
	803	Timothy Lawler,	Michael Walsh,	Hubbenstown,
	804	John Finelet,	do.	Grangefield,
	805	Philip Kinsella,	do.	Ballyvane,
	806	Michael Hickey,	Marquis of Drogheda,	Richardstown,
	807	Do.	do.	Myshallstown (term)
	808	Michael Donoghue,	do.	Cloneyburg,
	809	Michael Hickey,	do.	Haristown,
	810	Thomas Carroll,	do.	Clonyogah,
	811	James Dowling,	do.	Cloghran,
	812	Do.	do.	Moynaletraun,
B. R. Kays (Legal). S. Mourell. F. Callan.	813	Patrick J. Dunne,	Very Rev. Thomas Hunn,	Oldtown,
	814	Do.	do.	Kilcongbung,
	815	Do.	do.	Oldtown,
	816	Do.	do.	do.
B. R. Kays (Legal). A. S. Drane. F. Callan.	817	Patrick Monahan, contd. in name of James Monahan.	Peter Van Hewrigh,	Coortybille,
	818	Lucy Kelly,	Anne T. O'Sullivan, contd. in name of Daniel O'Sullivan.	Butterstream,

KILDARE—*continued.*

Extent of Holdings. Acres.	Poor Law Valuation.	Former Rent.	Judicial Rent.	Observations.
A. R. P.	£ s. d.	£ s. d.	£ s. d.	
7 1 61	3 10 0	3 0 0	3 13 0	
6 3 85	5 10 0	7 3 10	5 5 0	
5 1 56	5 70 0	5 5 0	5 10 0	
94 3 39	84 0 0	29 5 1	34 0 0	
11 3 37	14 6 0	79 0 0	15 0 0	
7 2 81	9 15 0	5 0 0	3 15 0	
36 3 76	16 10 0	31 0 0	30 0 0	
80 3 56	61 0 0	45 0 0	27 10 0	
54 0 0	61 0 0	54 0 0	16 10 0	
13 5 0	9 10 0	18 0 0	10 0 0	
11 3 32	9 0 0	11 0 0	10 0 0	
13 1 36	10 0 0	16 10 0	10 10 0	
9 3 7	6 0 0	5 0 0	4 0 0	
27 0 36	11 9 0	16 0 0	13 0 0	
44 2 33	19 9 0	17 5 7	17 5 7	
73 1 90	33 6 0	41 5 0	64 0 0	
90 3 22	45 10 0	61 0 0	40 0 0	
15 1 35	9 10 0	10 5 5	7 15 0	
5 0 14	1 15 0	5 19 9	3 10 9	
3 0 2	7 0 0	13 7 8	13 5 0	
19 2 30	13 17 0	15 0 0	38 30 0	
77 3 13	44 0 0	57 0 0	43 0 0	
11 0 5	10 15 0	23 0 0	10 5 0	
72 3 39	59 15 0	63 0 0	73 0 0	
33 0 38	29 0 0	27 10 0	24 0 0	By consent.
5 2 0	3 10 0	4 15 0	3 10 0	do.

Name of Assistant Commissioners by whom Cases were decided.	No.	Name of Tenant.	Name of Landlord.
Assistant Commissioners—			
R. R. MAUD (Legal). F. CALLAN .	619	James Martin, as alleged in name of Eleanor Martin.	Sir Arthur P. F. Ayl..
	620	Anne J. Johnston, —	do. —
	621	Francis Colgan and anor.,	Thomas Rawle and an..
	622	Do., ... —	Thomas Rawle and an..
	623	Allan Whyte, —	Francis W. Browne,
	624	Mathew Gill, ...	do. ...
	625	Patrick Watson, —	do. —
	626	Ellen Maher, with of Michael Maher.	James Mooney, ... name of James Mo..
	627	Mary Kennedy, minister	Major Hugh L. Bart..

KILDARE—continued.

Extent of Holding Statute.	Poor Law Valuation.	Former Rent.	Judicial Rent.	Observations.	Value of Tenancy.
A. R. P.	£ s. d.	£ s. d.	£ s. d.		£ s. d.
45 1 35	54 0 0	80 0 0	62 0 0		
18 0 0	10 10 0	18 0 0	13 10 0		
15 0 12	uncertained.	27 0 0	21 0 0		
68 2 3	do.	123 0 0	90 0 0		
91 1 35	63 15 0	67 10 0	56 0 0		
17 1 30	18 15 0	11 5 6	10 0 0		
54 3 19	41 10 0	67 8 10	35 0 0		
1 3 5	2 15 0	5 10 0	4 15 0		
1 3 33	5 0 0	1 3 0	2 5 0		
4 1 5	3 0 0	6 0 1	3 15 0		
1,271 1 19	1,058 10 0	1,513 6 3	1,913 1 4		

KILKENNY.

17 0 0	uncertained.	7 0 0	6 0 0		
152 3 18	56 0 0	46 0 0	45 0 0		
15 3 27	21 0 0	33 8 0	27 0 0		
3 3 11	1 10 0	3 0 0	5 0 0		
57 3 11	80 5 0	54 13 0	29 0 0		
30 3 18	11 10 0	14 15 0	7 10 0		
17 0 33	5 15 0	5 0 0	6 0 0		
0 1 1	2 10 0	3 11 9	2 5 0		
44 2 18	25 0 0	27 5 0	29 0 0		
9 3 14	5 0 0	9 0 0	5 5 0		
5 0 10	5 0 0	5 10 0	4 0 0		
24 3 14	18 15 0	15 5 0	10 10 0	90 0 0	
5 0 7	4 5 0	4 19 2	4 5 0	60 0 0	
16 3 0	13 15 0	17 7 10	13 10 0	50 0 0	

Named Assistant Commissioners by whom Claims were decided.	No.	Name of Tenant.	Name of Landlord.	Townland.
Assistant Commissioners—				
J. H. Edge (Legal). A. N. Cogan. J. H. Bryan.	2272	Martin Fitzgerald,	Rev. Dr. ... ..., vested in note of the Irish Land Commission,	Jamestown,
	2273	John Corr,	Earl of Dunraven,	Piercelands townshop, do.
	2274	Edward Corr,	do.	do.
	2275	Andrew Dillon,	do.	Cullinagarnra,
A. N. Cogan. J. H. Bryan.	2276	Robert Madigan,	Mrs. Anne J. Andrews,	Killbeis,
	2251	Thomas Kelly,	do.	Fishmore,
				Total,

Assistant Commissioners—				
M. T. Cogan (Legal). O. H. Miller. T. Davidson.	1889	Edward Carden,	Mrs. Mary A. Tyrell,	Carrick,
	1890	Joseph Morro,	Vincent Brickett and anr., Trustees of Marquis of Drumkisha,	Edenderry,
	1891	Bridget Flanagan, contd. in name of Mathew Flanagan.	Bernard Evans,	Derrygarran,
	1892	Mary McEvoy,	Thomas A. Gross,	O chow, Cornamona,
	1893	Thomas Muldoon,	R. D. Thompson, continued in name of Mary A. Thompson.	
	1894	Valentine Gaines,	do.	Clonmoylng,
				Total,

Assistant Commissioners—				
W. F. Bailey (Legal). F. O'Callaghan. L. J. Knoell.	2102	Thomas Flood,	William A. White,	Callanmore,
	2103	James Matterson,	Edward McEvoy,	Durragh,
				Total,

Photo of image digitised by the University of Southampton Library Digitisation Unit.

KILKENNY—*continued.*

Extent of Holding in Statute Acres	Poor Law Valuation.	Former Rent.	Judicial Rent.	Observations.	Value of Tenancy
A. R. P.	£ s. d.	£ s. d.	£ s. d.		£ s. d.
6 1 33	unascertained,	3 0 0	3 0 0		
138 2 29	99 10 0	99 0 9	83 0 0		
147 3 1	100 5 0	99 0 8	84 0 0		
118 1 22	101 0 0	04 0 0	87 0 0		
7 0 2	6 0 0	6 10 0	6 10 0		
18 5 25	12 0 0	15 0 0	13 10 0		
770 0 14	534 0 0	546 5 11	471 5 0		

COUNTY.

5 0 37	6 10 0	4 0 0	8 0 0		
86 1 8	25 0 0	83 0 0	22 0 0		
7 8 6	8 0 0	6 0 0	5 0 0		
231 0 1	26 5 0	30 0 0	85 0 0		
15 0 13	10 10 0	9 13 1	6 0 0		
10 0 30	8 0 0	7 4 0	4 0 0		
301 1 90	76 5 0	84 17 8	68 0 0		

LONGFORD.

COUNTY OF

Name of Judicial Commissioner by whom Case was decided.	No.	Name of Tenant.	Name of Landlord.	Townland.
Assistant Commissioners— W. F. Bailey (Legal). J. B. Hammer. G. N. Thompson	1498	Patrick Kearney,	John D. Bell,	Kinlin,
	1499	Thomas McCormick,	Lieut-Colonel J. C. W. Fortescue, committee in course of Captain, &c., Fortescue, &c.	Kilderroole,
	1519	Kate Murray,	do.	Clonmagoolil,
	1671	Patrick Kearney,	Joseph A. Conlinn,	Rathkeelland map
	1271	Mary Revell,	Timothy P. H. M. Filgate,	Pleaner,
	1472	Luke Traynor,	Arthur J. Howell,	Ballyheenocke,
	1473	Fanny Silli,	A. Howell,	Derryballen,
	1575	John Kielly,	Daniel Kelly,	Homestown,
	1576	John Charles,	Lord Ouddingford,	Drumaklin,
	1477	Mary Moore,	do.	Ranksmarshall,
				Total,

COUNTY OF

Head Commissioner.	1568	Patrick Cuddy,	Marquis Conyngham,	Conmore,
	1569	Patrick Wall,	do.	Davidstown and another.
W. E. Bailey (Legal). F. O'Hagan. L. J. Hanna.	1570	Patrick Nevill, senior,	William Thompson,	Moulin,
	1571	Patrick Nevill, junior,	do.	do.
	1572	Jane Neville,	do.	do.
	1573	Francis Gorman,	do.	Maynad,
	1574	John Geraghty, Rep. of Nicholas Geraghty.	Rev. William A. Nevile,	Middleborough,
	1575	James Jiles,	do.	Moylin,
	1576	Richard Reynolds,	Rev. Thomas Allen,	Maxorhead,
	1577	Patrick Regan,	do.	do.
	1578	Joseph Greville,	Robert Fowler,	Leamstown,
W. E. Bailey (Legal). T. Marshall. G. N. Thompson.	1579	Mary McDermott,	Marquis of Headfort,	Mast,
	1580	Robert Porter,	do.	Curragh,

11	10	0	13	2	8
57	5	0	64	18	0
45	15	0	48	10	0
600	0	0	519	5	5
5	5	0	10	0	0
50	5	0	23	6	9
16	10	0	18	0	0
19	0	0	16	0	0
70	5	0	73	15	5
44	10	0	61	11	8
43	10	0	51	5	0
31	5	0	55	12	0

COUNTY OF

Names of Assistants Commissioners by whom Cases were decided.	No.	Name of Tenant.	Name of Landlord.	Townland.
Assistant Commissioners— R. R. Kane (Legal). E. Mowbray. R. Martin.	1883	James Dunne,	Edward Woods,	Byrnestown,
B. R. Kane (Legal). E. Mowbray.	1884	Mary McKee,	Nathaniel P. Preston,	KCest, Total,

QUEEN'S

Head Commissioner.	1729	James Behan,	Cornelia Adair,	Rathlair,
	1783	Mrs. Marks Behan,	do.	do.
Assistant Commissioners— R. R. Kane (Legal). W. S. Hyde. E. Martin.	1784	Andrew Brennan,	Rev. George W. Grogan,	Fallaghmore,
J. H. Finn (Legal). L. Cleary. B. H. Prumla.	1785	Joseph Wallwood,	Colonel William Dacier,	Lisbigney,
	1786	John Creevy,	Joseph Carter,	Ballypickas,
	1787	Thomas Kelly,	William Owen, continued in name of Arthur J. Owen.	Gartows,
	1788	John Gallagher,	Edward H. Brooke,	Ardlea, Total,

COUNTY OF

Assistant Commissioners— R. R. Kane (Legal). C. R. Butler. H. E. Stannus.	1792	Mrs. Anne Russell,	Dame Leitita Nugent,	Walshestown, Sth.
	1796	John Donelan,	do.	do.
	1787	Ellen Byrne,	do.	do.
	1798	Christopher Cowan,	Lord Dongloven	Glomen,
	1799	Robert Roe,	Cornelia R. Sarode, continued	Glenabbin,

MEATH—*continued.*

Name of Holding, Occupier.	Poor Law Valuation.	Former Rent.	Judicial Rent.	Observations.
A. R. P.	£ s. d.	£ s. d.	£ s. d.	
63 3 33	75 10 0	81 0 9	75 0 0	

Names of Assistant-Commissioners by whom Court was desired.	No.	Name of Tenant.	Name of Landlord.	Townland.
Assistant Commissioners:—				
R. R. Bane (Legal),	1751	John Moran,	Mrs. G. Molyneux,	Roderigh,
C. B. Bowman,	1752	Bridget Garty,	Lord Carville,	Clonmurry,
H. E. Hearons.	1753	John Henry,	Lady E. Beckworth,	Fulnard,
	1754	Francis Davison,	do.	do.
	1755	Patrick Gowran,	do.	do.
	1756	Do.	do.	do.
	1757	Do.	do.	do.
	1758	Myles McClellan,	do.	do.
	1759	Ellen Lyons,	Peter Murray,	Killinick,
	1760	John Gill,	do.	do.
	1761	John Murray,	do.	Delgahara,
	1762	John Gowran,	Colonel Andrew Nugent,	Dysart,
	1763	Richard Bond,	Mrs. R. J. Bond, as administratrix of William P. Bond,	Derry,
	1764	Mary Elbert and sons,	John Mullins,	Ballishen,
	1765	James Drew,	do.	do.
	1766	Elizabeth Kenny,	William J. Parry,	Kinaliginshin,
	1767	Bernard Corcoran,	Mrs. Bess Warburton,	Cloonetlacigh,
	1768	Mrs. Anne G. Gantrell, as tenant of Amelia Present,	do.	Cloonetlacigh and adjoining,
	1769	Ellen Leary,	Thomas McNeal,	Eskragh,
	1770	Mathew Finnehan,	do.	do.
	1771	Michael Mallery,	Michael Finion,	Ballynamullagh,
	1772	Thomas Nally, sued in name of Margaret Nally,	Major R. H. Rochfort Boyd, sued in name of Geo. W. Derwent Moore and son,	do.
	1773	Richard Wallace,	do.	Biggenhern and another,
	1774	Thomas Gowran,	do.	Rathmullagh,
	1775	Catherine Kinnan,	do.	do.
	1776	James Killian,	do.	do.
	1777	Richard Hardie,	John E. Bransford,	Glenfield,
	1778	Patrick Finnegan,	do.	do.
	1779	Pat Conway, sued in name of John Conway,	do.	do.
	1780	William Cunningham,	do.	do.
	1781	Thomas Farrell,	do.	do.
	1782	Thomas Clayton,	do.	do.
	1783	Thomas Whelan,	do.	do.

Printed image digitised by the University of Southampton Library Digitisation Unit.

WESTMEATH—continued.

Extent of Holding. Roods.	Poor Law Valuation.	Former Rent.	Judicial Rent.	Observations.
A. R. P.	£ s. d.	£ s. d.	£ s. d.	
5 0 16	9 10 0	4 4 0	5 5 0	
13 1 20	15 10 0	25 10 4	19 10 8	
6 0 15	5 10 0	5 0 0	4 13 0	
15 0 30	17 10 5	16 0 0	17 0 0	
11 0 16	6 18 0	11 0 0	9 8 0	
5 2 9	4 0 0	5 0 0	4 6 0	
17 2 5	5 10 0	11 0 0	9 17 0	
25 1 30	28 10 0	25 0 0	21 5 0	
1 2 19	1 0 0	1 4 0	0 12 0	
4 2 0	2 0 0	2 0 0	2 0 0	
3 1 27	1 5 0	1 0 0	1 0 0	
13 2 5	10 15 0	12 0 0	10 0 0	
52 0 10	57 4 0	59 11 11	51 0 0	
61 1 19	59 0 0	66 15 8	56 0 0	
18 0 0	11 5 0	9 7 5	5 15 0	
20 1 9	12 7 0	16 0 0	11 5 0	
16 5 0	5 0 0	5 5 0	4 15 0	
156 3 7	195 15 0	179 10 0	136 0 0	
4 1 0	2 5 0	5 5 0	2 5 0	
3 3 20	1 5 0	5 1 5	1 12 0	
1 2 23	5 10 0	1 5 0	1 5 0	
80 1 25	16 15 0	22 10 0	19 10 0	
75 0 6	51 5 0	57 7 10	28 10 0	
18 2 29	17 10 0	18 0 0	17 0 0	
107 5 14	55 0 0	75 0 0	65 0 0	
101 0 13	53 5 0	45 0 0	51 0 0	
45 5 4	16 10 5	15 17 0	15 15 0	
18 1 0	5 0 0	5 0 0	5 5 0	
25 5 27	10 0 0	10 4 0	5 5 0	
20 1 30	5 14 0	7 10 0	5 15 0	
19 2 0	5 10 0	5 1 0	5 5 0	
15 0 15	4 5 0	3 14 5	3 14 5	
7 0 5	5 10 0	2 3 5	2 2 5	

COUNTY OF

Names of Assistant Commissioners by whom Cases were decided.	No.	Name of Tenant.	Name of Landlord.	Townland.
Assistant Commissioners— R. R. Kane (Legal). C. R. Barton. H. B. Sharman.	1765	Thomas Hughes, ...	John F. Bamford, ...	Clonfad, ...
	1766	Mary Ryan, Admin. of Bridget Ryan.	John A. McConchy and others, Assignees of Sir W. Nugent, a bankrupt.	Newtown and another.
	1767	Elizabeth Ward, ...	do.	Castletown, ...
	1768	Thomas M. Reddy, ...	John Connell, ...	Cullenmore, ...
	1769	John Kiernan, ...	Major R. Murphy, ...	Ballydillagh, ...
	1770	Mrs. Ellen Coffey, ...	do.	Taghens, ...
	1771	Michael Brown, ...	Henry C. Levinge, ...	Culleen Beg, ...
	1772	James Nolan, ...	do.	do. ...
	1773	Andrew Maguire, ...	do.	Culleen, ...
	1774	Thomas Tuite, ...	do.	do. ...
	1775	Margaret Shaw, ...	do.	Cullenbeg, ...
	1776	Peter Devlin, ...	do.	Knockaville, ...
	1777	Mathew Nugent, ...	do.	Rathloo, ...
	1778	Elizabeth Ward, ...	Earl of Longford, ...	Castletown, ...
	1779	John Keenan, ...	do.	Castledown, ...
	1780	Julia Gallagher, Admin. of Thomas Gallagher and another.	Mrs. Emily Tyrrell, ...	[illegible] Tyrrell.
	1781	Margaret Lacey, Admin. of Thomas Lacey.	Captain L. Murphy, ...	Lackanwood. ...
	1782	John Kim, ...	Captain Ralph Smythe, continued in name of Colonel James Smythe,	Glanelog, ...
	1783	Joseph Clarke, ...	Captain R. W. Boyd-Rochfort, sued in name of Capt. W. L. [illegible] & anor.	Rathconnellbeagh,
	1784	Catherine Kiernan, ...	do.	do. ...
	1785	Mary Anne Hemingbrough, continued in name of John Fox.	do.	do. ...
				Total, ...

Acres of Holding Drawn.	Poor Law Valuation.	Former Rent.	Judicial Rent.	Observations.	Value of Tenancy.
A. R. P.	£ s. d.	£ s. d.	£ s. d.		£ s. d.
5 6 27	2 9 0	8 10 0	5 10 0		
8 0 20	—	8 13 8	9 10 0		
48 1 0	48 0 0	44 0 9	46 0 0		
3 0 0	7 0 0	3 0 0	2 0 0		
1 4 20	4 10 0	3 0 0	3 7 0		
20 1 0	16 0 0	13 2 8	16 13 8		
7 0 10	3 8 0	5 11 0	4 8 0		
61 1 15	13 10 0	13 6 0	11 5 0		
33 8 0	18 0 0	21 0 0	17 10 0		
16 1 15	7 15 0	6 5 0	7 0 0		
101 1 0	37 10 0	45 9 0	40 0 0		
23 3 26	16 0 0	21 0 0	20 0 0		
43 3 53	29 10 0	33 0 0	25 10 0		
9 1 36	9 0 0	10 0 0	9 0 0		
100 0 0	55 10 0	63 0 0	48 0 0		
45 1 4	25 10 0	44 8 0	38 0 0		
38 2 27	25 0 0	27 0 0	30 0 0		
18 1 0	14 18 0	15 4 4	16 8 0		
16 0 15	9 10 0	10 0 0	8 16 0		
325 0 25	165 0 0	215 0 0	217 0 0		
20 3 17	22 5 0	88 0 0	21 5 0		
2,145 3 25	1,237 16 0	1,818 5 5	1,317 18 2		

IRISH LAND COMMISSION.

COUNTY OF

Provisional Assistant Commissioners by whom Cases were Certified.	No.	Name of Townland.	Name of Landlord.	Barony.
Assistant Commissioners—				
J. H. Enss (Legal).	2183	Margaret Leary,	Count de Raymond,	Glenraughty,
M. F. Lynch.	2184	Thomas Watkins,	Joseph Watkins,	Kilmaline,
W. Wallace.	2185	Charles Nolan,	Rev. Michael Vaney,	Cadran,
	2186	William Ryon,	William J. Kingan,	Ballywattacash,
	2187	Thomas Robertson,	John A. Macaulay and others, Assignees of William Bolton, a Bankrupt.	Ballyrainey,
	2188	John Somerset,	John F. Leahy,	Cashes,
	2189	James Stafford,	Captain Standish O'Grady and another.	Ballyrainoff,
	2170	John Morrison,	M. E. Darcy, seized, in trust of W. F. McEvoy,	Ballynakill,
	2171	John Charlton,	Rev. W. G. Ormsby,	Kilteddy,
	2172	Karms Neill,	Sylvester Neill,	Newtown,
	2113	Morgan Devine,	Lord Cloete,	Knockmore,
	2174	James Whitty,	do.	Tumbelok,
	2175	Margaret Megan,	Luther A. Bryan,	Clogh,
	2176	John H. W. Sterling,	do.	Ballieglisey,
	2177	James Leary,	Matthew Leary,	Clesinga,
	2178	Margaret Pierce,	Earl of Courtown,	Ologry,
	2179	Francis M. Kingh,	do.	do.
	2180	Taggt Neill,	do.	do.
	2181	J. H. W. Sterling,	do.	Ballaoghton,
	2182	George Cooper,	do.	Millockogan,
	2183	Michael Neill,	Samuel J. Squire and others,	Ballymaney,
	2184	John Doran,	do.	do.
				Total,

COUNTY OF

HEAD COMMISSIONER.	1090	Henry Chapman,	Robert G. Wade and another,	Thomasdown,
R. B. Kavs (Legal).	1091	John Byrne,	Peter Kelly,	Cooladoyle,
W. G. Dz Lt Poer.	1092	Patrick Stephens,	Thomas Heaton,	Downhill,
J. Hawksworth.	1093	Elizabeth Woodruffe,	William Kenvale,	Rahenamett,
	1094	William L. Barns,	Thomas Arbuth,	Milesroad.

WEXFORD—*continued.*

Extent of Holdings. Boards.	Poor Law Valuation.	Former Rent.	Judicial Rent.	Observations.	Value of Tenancy.
A. R. P.	£ s. d.	£ s. d.	£ s. d.		£ s. d.
17 0 1	13 10 0	14 10 0	13 0 0		
6 1 37	3 10 0	4 15 0	5 0 0		
81 3 10	2 15 0	10 0 0	8 13 0		
53 1 32	23 0 0	25 4 0	17 10 0		
8 1 10	2 10 0	5 9 4	2 5 0		
73 0 19	16 15 0	17 3 6	14 10 0		
73 1 87	63 15 0	75 14 0	59 0 0		
105 1 15	63 3 0	75 0 0	50 5 9		
83 0 11	13 5 0	20 0 0	14 0 0		
1 0 84	0 15 0	1 10 0	0 15 0		
43 2 0	18 15 0	51 15 11	15 10 0		
54 1 33	28 15 0	25 0 0	23 10 0		
4 0 10	3 10 0	4 9 3	3 4 0		
87 3 33	50 0 0	59 11 4	43 0 0		
4 1 5	1 15 0	2 15 0	1 10 0		
71 0 16	58 0 0	53 9 0	41 10 0		
30 0 15	13 10 0	14 0 0	14 0 0		
38 0 34	20 10 0	27 15 4	18 0 0		
62 3 11	43 10 0	48 5 0	45 5 0		
133 0 7	48 0 0	55 0 0	48 0 0		
10 1 37	11 15 0	14 8 0	10 0 0		
60 1 0	23 0 0	25 0 0	25 5 0		
1,034 5 5	571 15 0	647 11 11	418 15 10		

WICKLOW.

17 1 19	19 15 0	21 0 0	14 0 0	The rent in this case was fixed by consent of the parties at the sitting of the Court in Dublin.	
93 2 1	17 15 0	45 0 0	24 10 0		
34 3 61	6 10 0	16 7 0	13 10 0		
87 0 5	29 10 0	55 15 4	13 0 0		
105 3 35	53 5 0	70 0 0	48 0 0		

Printed image donated by the University of Southampton Library Digitisation Unit

F 2

IRISH LAND COMMISSION.

Names of Assistant Commissioners by whom Cases were decided.	No.	Name of Tenant.	Name of Landlord.	Townland.
Assistant Commissioners—				
R. R. Kane (Legal). W. G. De la Poer. J. Haverty.	1093	Jeremiah Arthurs,	C. E. Guy Cunningham,	Newtown,
	1095	Robert Blair, senial, administrator of Patrick Tylan,	do.	Hawkistown,
	1097	Kate Flynn, administratrix of James Flynn,	do.	Newtown Mount kennedy,
	1098	Do.	do.	do.
	1099	Robert Ball,	do.	do.
	1100	Do.	do.	Kilmacullagh,
	1101	James Hopekirk,	do.	Kilpedder, East,
	1102	Kate Flynn, administratrix of James Flynn,	do.	Newtown Mount kennedy,
	1103	Robert Ball,	do.	Kilmacullagh,
	1104	Do.	do.	Kilpedder,
	1105	Do.	do.	Kilmacullagh,
	1106	Denis Keane,	Henry Sluggish,	Kyleabeloro,
	1107	John Redmond,	do.	Kilbeccanaghmore, Ballinabarney,
	1108	William Manley,	William W. F. Dick,	Ballinabarney,
	1109	Mathew Farrell,	do.	Ballyguananea,
	1110	George Golden, junior,	do.	Carrowtown,
	1111	George Golden, senior,	do.	do.
	1112	James Flinn,	do.	Ballyguananea, Tuck,

PROVINCE OF

WICKLOW—*continued.*

Extent of Holding. Statute.	Poor Law Valuation.	Former Rent.	Judicial Rent.	Observations.	Value of Tenancy.
A. R. P.	£ s. d.	£ s. d.	£ s. d.		£ s. d.
64 0 29	43 0 0	69 16 10	38 16 10		
71 0 22	83 0 0	64 19 0	67 0 0		
8 0 25	6 8 0	16 6 0	9 0 0		
4 0 85	8 0 0	11 0 0	8 0 0		
8 1 0	5 4 0	6 0 0	4 16 0		
3 1 24	11 0 0	16 0 0	11 10 0		
12 2 14	19 0 0	33 0 0	18 0 0		
15 0 30	15 15 0	23 0 0	16 4 0		
3 1 17	2 10 0	6 5 0	8 0 0		
43 1 28	71 6 0	107 0 0	68 0 0		
1 2 0	3 15 0	6 0 0	8 10 0		
33 1 0	26 16 0	26 15 0	13 0 0		
84 2 24	48 0 0	66 10 0	48 0 0		
42 0 0	25 10 0	29 0 0	19 0 0		
70 1 31	37 10 0	69 12 7	32 0 0		
51 2 0	22 0 0	25 0 0	21 0 0		
51 3 0	12 0 0	25 0 0	23 0 0		
43 3 29	21 0 0	30 0 0	21 0 0		
711 1 16	496 8 0	778 5 6	547 11 10		

CONNAUGHT.

GALWAY.

Names of Assistant Commissioners by whom Cases were decided.	No.	Name of Tenant.	Name of Landlord.
Assistant Commissioners—			
M. T. Brady (Legal).	8571	Mark Calkin,	Joseph M. Fielden,
R. McCabe.	8572	Patrick Halfdine,	Alliance Assurance Coy.
A. R. Montgomery.	8573	Patrick Burrell,	do.
	8574	Patrick Healy,	Mrs. Mary Shaftesbury,
	8575	Michael Heston,	John McCready,
	8576	John Howell, junior,	John Byrne,
	8577	Bartholomew Elwood,	do.
	8578	John Darley,	Major J. DeB. Lydick,
	8579	John Martin,	Mrs. Jane C. D'Arcy,
	8580	Bridget Burke,	John O'Flaherty,
	8581	John O'Donnell,	F. J. Blake,
	8582	Michael Blake,	do.
	8583	Mary Collins, (del. of William Collins)	Colonel Timothy Burke,
	8584	Richard Burke,	do.
	8585	Catherine Dunphy,	John A. Brown,
	8586	John Daisy,	do.
	8587	James White,	do.
	8588	Denis Gallagher,	do.
	8589	Francis Fanning, Ltd., (extr. of Michael Fanning)	do.
	8590	Patrick Byrne,	Dolores Joplin,
	8591	Bridget Fahy,	do.
	8592	Michael Byrne,	do.
	8593	Martin Brennan,	do.
	8594	James Fahy,	do.
	8595	Patrick Connolly,	do.

GALWAY—*continued.*

Extent of Holding. Stat.	Poor Law Valuation.	Former Rent.	Judicial Rent.	Observations.	Value of Tenancy.
A. R. P.	£ s. d.	£ s. d.	£ s. d.		£ s. d.
68 1 0	17 10 0	25 0 0	19 10 0		
34 3 10	6 10 0	8 10 0	4 16 0		
19 0 34	5 6 0	6 0 0	4 15 0		
9 0 12	3 18 0	5 10 0	6 13 4		
104 3 0	77 10 0	20 0 8	80 0 0		
4 3 3	2 13 0	3 7 0	2 0 0		
17 3 4	5 5 0	6 7 0	5 13 0		
3 1 13	1 10 0	1 13 0	1 5 0		
57 3 1	8 10 0	5 0 0	8 0 0		
70 2 30	16 10 0	73 3 10	13 0 0		
7 1 30	5 0 0	5 0 3	8 15 0	Right of commonage with 5 others over 573 acres. do.	
17 3 0	3 3 0	7 5 3	5 5 0		
32 0 37	16 10 0	10 9 8	15 10 0		
6 3 3	5 15 0	5 5 0	5 0 0		
31 3 31	unascertained.	4 10 0	3 5 0		
37 3 3	do.	3 15 0	3 0 0		
7 0 1	3 0 0	6 0 0	8 5 0		
7 3 0	unascertained.	6 0 0	6 0 0		
31 3 30	do.	3 0 0	1 10 0		
9 0 22	13 0 0	16 1 0	10 10 0		
6 0 33	13 10 0	16 1 0	10 10 0		
6 3 37	5 0 0	6 0 3	3 3 0		
9 3 3	13 0 0	14 1 0	10 10 0		
6 0 16	13 3 0	16 3 0	10 10 0		
5 0 1	15 0 0	33 1 0	10 10 0		
30 3 13	15 0 0	33 10 0	13 0 0		
6 3 35	unascertained.	3 3 0	3 0 0		
3 0 19	do.	3 10 0	1 16 0		
34 0 7	do.	11 0 0	7 5 0		
9 3 32	5 0 0	4 1 0	3 10 0		
35 1 27	3 15 0	11 19 3	9 10 0		
9 0 34	3 5 0	6 0 0	3 10 0		
31 1 30	5 10 0	11 0 0	7 13 0		
13 3 34	3 10 0	3 13 0	6 10 0		
6 3 1	3 5 0	4 10 0	3 17 8		

Name of Judicial Commissioners by whom Cases were decided.	No.	Name of Tenant.	Name of Landlord.	Townland.
Assistant Commissioners—				
M. T. OMAR (Legal).	8605	Thomas Flaherty,	Francis L. Court,	Corriston,
R. McCALL.	8607	Michael Corbett,	do.	do.
A. R. MONTGOMERY.	8608	Mattie Cassels,	do.	do.
	8609	Martin Walsh,	Captain R. W. Morris,	Gortnamona,
	8612	Patrick Walsh,	Margaret McGee,	Oriston, Bog,
	8611	Do.,	James Gibbons,	do.
	8612	John Madden,	James F. Wright,	Cappaquill,
	8613	do.,	Henry Edmiston,	Gortmore,
	8614	Patrick Newell,	Rev. R. W. Turner and others, Trustees of Richard Liversidge, deceased,	Carrandulla,
	8615	John Gannon,	Mrs. Eliza Burke,	Cloonbigeen,
	8616	Patrick Walsh, Ltd. Administ. of Thomas Walsh,	George E. O'Flaherty,	Ambroseile,
	8617	Peter O'Malley,	Colonel H. T. Clements,	Brimmore,
	8618	Do.,	do.,	Killadillo,
	8619	Patrick Mannix,	Lord Ardilaun,	Ballynahinch,
	8620	Martin Stansfield, Rep. of Thomas Stansfield,	do.	Renvees, East and another.
	8621	Michael Joyce, junior,	do.	Renvyle,
	8622	Patrick Lydon,	Thomas H. Ogle,	Birrisleigh,
	8623	Healy King,	Richard Kearney,	Oreep,
	8624	John Clancey,	do.	do.
	8625	Tom Connelly,	do.	do.
	8626	Peter Walsh,	do.	do.
	8627	Thomas Flynn,	do.	do.
	8628	Michael King,	do.	Claddaghduff,
	8629	Pat Coohan,	do.	Orney Island,
	8630	John Lynn,	Charles Lydon,	Cloonkdura,
J. S. OMAN, Q.C. (Legal).	8631	James Flaherty,	Robert T. K. St. George and another,	Cartron,
W. O HETT.	8632	Edward Meenaghin,	Thomas E. Liddiff, a lunatic, by J. R. Liddiff, His Committee,	Ballyban,
H. C. NAG.	8633	William Cahir,	do.	do.
	8634	Mattie Mayes,	do.	do.
	8635	Bridget Nicholson, Rep. of James Nicholson,	do.	Cloganbolla,
	8636	Patrick Niblad (Pat),	Very Rev. Dean West,	Barrleigh,
	8637	Pat Kilhale (John),	do.	do.

GALWAY—*continued.*

Name of Holdings Occupier.	Poor Law Valuation.	Former Rent.	Judicial Rent.	Observations.	Table of Tenancy
a. r. p.	£ s. d.	£ s. d.	£ s. d.		£ s. d.
5 2 4	1 5 9	2 13 6	1 16 0		
b 3 27	3 6 8	3 13 6	2 5 6		
2 3 3	3 9 7	4 12 6	3 9 6		
1 1 9	0 15 0	2 0 0	0 15 0		
1 1 18	unascertained	1 0 0	0 15 0		
1 3 2	do.	1 0 0	0 15 0		
20 0 23	18 0 0	18 0 0	13 10 0		
45 1 25	18 0 0	27 0 0	20 0 0		
17 1 9	8 10 0	9 10 0	8 10 0		
9 0 20	1 0 0	4 0 0	3 5 0	Together with right of grazing two cattle on mountain.	
4 1 10	3 11 0	5 0 0	3 5 0	Together with right of grazing three cattle on mountain.	
101 1 11	60 0 0	75 5 0	57 0 0		
30 1 11	11 10 0	15 14 0	10 10 0		
41 2 21	20 0 0	20 0 0	20 10 0		
17 2 16	2 0 0	13 2 6	1 5 0		
35 3 31	2 10 0	1 15 0	2 10 0	Right of grazing with four others over 15a., as Bridget Mannion.	
unascertained	3 15 0	4 10 0	3 10 0	do.	
4 0 0	7 0 0	3 8 5	2 0 0	do.	
7 0 0	2 0 0	2 0 8	1 0 0	do.	
4 0 0	2 0 0	3 6 8	2 0 0	do.	
2 0 0	2 0 0	3 6 8	2 0 0	do.	
2 0 0	unascertained	3 6 0	2 0 0	do.	
3 0 0	do.	2 12 0	1 0 0	do.	
4 0 0	1 0 0	3 6 7	2 0 0	do.	
2 0 0	1 15 0	2 5 0	2 12 6	do.	

Names of Assistant Commissioners by whom Cases were decided.	No.	Name of Tenant.	Name of Landlord.
Assistant Commissioners— J. R. Ormsby, &c. (Legal). W. R. Hoyte. H. C. Bath.	8838	John Niland,	Very Rev. Dean West,
	8839	Catherine Niland,	do. —
	8840	William Connors,	do. —
	8841	Michael Cassidy,	do. —
	8842	Mary Connors,	do. —
	8843	John Connors,	do. —
	8844	Winifred Connors,	do. —
	8845	Honor Connors,	do. —
	8846	Denis Mahon,	do. —
	8847	Peter Clonnan,	do. —
	8848	Laurence Niland,	do. —
	8849	Pat Purdo,	do. —
	8850	Bridget Martyn,	do. —
	8851	Denis Niland,	do. —
	8852	John Carey and another,	Edward Hartigan,
	8853	John Hand,	Richard Galbraith,
	8854	Archibald R. Hearn,	Major-General W. R. C
	8854	Lizzie Joyce,	do. —
	8856	George Logan,	F. C. Sampson, a mi

Extent of Holdings Acres			Poor Law Valuation			Former Rent			Judicial Rent		
A.	R.	P.	£	s.	d.	£	s.	d.	£	s.	d.
51	3	18	14	10	8	17	0	6	11	19	0
26	1	31	11	0	0	13	0	0	8	0	0
16	0	17	8	0	0	8	15	0	6	0	0
40	0	14	13	10	0	13	0	0	9	0	0
44	2	7	13	10	0	14	3	0	9	0	0
24	1	7	6	5	0	8	0	8	8	0	8
16	0	31	4	0	8	5	0	8	3	0	0
16	0	35	4	0	0	8	6	0	3	0	0
38	1	13	8	0	0	11	9	0	7	18	0
13	3	37	9	13	0	10	0	0	8	0	0
34	3	25	23	13	3	28	8	3	13	0	0
84	3	10	13	0	0	28	0	0	14	0	0
84	0	15	17	10	0	30	0	0	14	0	0
24	1	30	13	10	0	16	0	0	10	0	0
48	1	17	unvalued			13	0	0	8	0	0
51	3	6	8	5	0	8	0	8	4	0	0
18	1	30	8	6	0	7	0	0	4	0	0
6	1	31	1	8	0	5	10	0	4	0	0
8	0	0	3	13	0	4	0	0	8	0	0
1	3	10	2	0	0	6	0	0	3	0	0
64	3	6	33	5	0	37	0	0	25	10	0
33	3	0	16	13	0	21	5	3	14	10	0
43	0	0	33	0	0	34	0	0	17	0	0
63	0	33	8	0	0	10	1	0	6	0	0
44	1	7	13	0	0	30	0	0	10	10	0
60	0	37	14	0	0	18	13	6	11	0	0
4	0	8	3	7	0	5	3	0	1	13	0
75	0	31	51	8	0	43	6	3	31	0	0
13	1	13	unvalued			10	11	6	6	13	7
34	3	23	18	13	0	18	0	0	15	0	0
64	7	0	44	18	0	50	4	0	44	10	0
148	1	0	7	13	0	8	5	0	6	3	0

Parties of Accounts Complainance by whom Costs were decided.	No.	Name of Tenant.	Name of Landlord.	Townland.
Assistant Commissioners:— M. R. Guran (Legal), J. T. Dwyer, B., Trimm.	5571	John Kennedy, contd. in name of John Galvin,	Sir Henry G. Burke, Bart.,	Bridge Park and others
	5572	Patrick Moynahan, ...	Charles G. Blake,	Breakhrombeg, —
	5573	Bridget Rabbitt, Limtd. Admin. of Catharine Rabbitt,	Jordan Horan, —	Ballingarry.
	5574	Thomas Donnolly, ...	Mrs. Kate Graham and anon.	Grinaga,
	5575	Patrick Connolly, ...	Dermot O'G. Dennick, contd. in name of Elizabeth Dennehan.	Garroon, —
	5576	John Higgins, Ltd. Admin. of Honoria Higgins.	Mariah S. Corcellis,	Ballingrene, —
	5577	John Carradom, ...	do. —	Upper Laskes, —
	5578	Bridget Hawkins, ...	do. —	do. —
	5579	Ellen Kelly, continued in name of Thomas Callinan.	do. —	Ballysagron, —
	5580	Thomas Donly, —	do. —	Upper Laskes and another.
	5581	Colin Marten, ...	R. G. Villiers, —	Clonash, —
	5582	Bridget Fallon, —	do. —	do.
	5583	Mary Menton, ...	do. —	do. —
	5584	Thomas Mitchell, ...	do. —	do. —
	5585	William Robinson, ...	Earl of Clancarty,	Shangarry, —
	5586	Benjamin Taylor, —	do. —	Caherroon, East.
	5587	Lawrence M. Egan, —	do. —	Lismahill, —
	5588	Michael O'Malla, ...	do. —	do. —
	5589	Edward Coy, ...	do. —	Barnagurrane, —
	5590	Catharine Cooke, Ltd. Admin. of Patrick Cooke.	do. —	do. —
	5591	Michael Lahy, ...	do. —	Caherntrim, —
	5592	Joseph Clarke, ...	do. —	Barnagurrane, —
	5593	John E. Mitchell, ...	do. —	Ballycanony, —
	5594	Catharine Quirke, Ltd. Admin. of James Quirke.	do. —	Caherroon, —
	5595	Michael Conroy, ...	Isabella M. Bevin,	Kilroon, —
	5596	John Kennedy, ...	do. —	do. —
	5597	John Lawlees, —	do. —	Ballydagan, —
	5598	Patrick Malony, —	do. —	do. —
	5599	Patrick Marvin, —	do. —	Kilroon, —
	5700	John Mealy, contd. in name of John Cahill.	do. —	Ballydagan, —
	5701	John Bane, ...	do. —	Kilroon, —

GALWAY—continued.

Amount of Letting, &c.	Poor Law Valuation.	Former Rent.	Judicial Rent.	Observations.
A. R. P.	£ s. d.	£ s. d.	£ s. d.	
23 1 35	33 5 0	47 0 0	52 10 6	
60 2 25	14 0 0	17 0 0	12 10 0	
20 1 35	10 10 0	17 0 0	11 0 0	
5 3 0	8 5 0	4 0 0	5 0 0	
34 3 5	34 5 0	24 0 0	16 0 0	
13 3 5	10 10 0	14 10 0	6 12 0	
14 2 7	11 0 0	22 4 10	9 0 0	
16 2 5	10 10 0	12 4 10	8 0 0	
44 3 57	unascertained,	55 19 5	27 15 0	
19 0 5	do.	17 11 0	10 0 0	
15 2 15	3 5 0	5 5 5	9 12 0	
35 2 0	5 0 0	5 15 0	5 2 0	
9 3 39	2 5 0	5 5 5	7 12 5	
9 3 30	unascertained,	7 9 5	5 5 0	
41 1 35	18 15 0	16 2 6	13 10 0	
23 2 0	15 0 0	19 5 0	18 10 5	
55 1 5	unascertained,	54 0 0	51 0 0	
40 0 34	16 15 0	22 11 2	19 10 0	
23 5 5	20 10 0	22 17 6	16 15 0	
50 2 5	22 5 0	25 2 2	17 10 6	
40 0 6	66 10 0	53 7 6	52 10 0	
10 0 17	5 0 0	9 0 0	6 5 0	
75 2 2	56 5 0	64 5 0	54 10 0	
11 3 25	8 15 0	10 0 0	8 5 0	
10 1 20	5 5 0	5 10 5	7 0 0	And ⅓ of commonage. 11s. 1s. 0r.
35 2 25	21 10 0	26 0 0	54 10 0	
25 0 35	14 0 0	14 0 0	14 0 0	
63 0 35	14 10 0	15 11 5	19 19 0	
50 0 19	15 10 0	30 5 5	15 0 6	
5 3 21	5 5 0	5 7 5	5 12 5	
5 1 5	5 0 0	5 17 10	5 10 0	And ⅛ undivided.

Assistant Commissioners:—

D. Turner (Legal).
C. U'Heztya.
B. Johnston.

4344	Pat McManus,	—	Mrs. Charlotte Irwin,
4345	Patrick Maguire,	. —	Thomas J. Norris,
4346	Hugh Conlan,	—	Colonel H. T. Clements,
4347	John Conlan,	—	do. —
4348	Francis McCabe,	—	do. —
4349	Anne Foley,	—	do. —
4350	Catherine Reynolds,	.. —	do. —
4351	Myles Shanly,	—	George Marsham,
4352	John Shanly, entd. in name of Pat Shanly.		do. —
4353	Thomas Harte,	..	do. —
4354	Michael Duignan,	—	do. —
4355	Michael Ryan,	...	Major W. H. White,

GALWAY—*continued.*

Extent of Holdings included	Poor Law Valuation	Former Rent	Judicial Rent	Observations
A. R. P.	£ s. d.	£ s. d.	£ s. d.	
19 0 37	5 10 0	6 7 0	6 0 0	
1 3 10	1 5 0	2 0 0	1 5 0	
25 3 10	9 10 0	16 3 0	9 13 0	
45 3 16	19 10 0	22 13 6	17 10 0	
4 1 7	4 5 0	6 0 0	5 7 6	
14 3 25	12 0 0	23 0 0	13 10 0	
57 0 30	57 10 0	34 15 10	39 15 0	
103 3 25	47 10 0	49 14 10	43 13 6	
11 3 5	3 5 0	6 11 1	4 13 0	
5 0 76	4 18 0	4 13 0	4 18 0	By agreement
66 3 0	27 10 0	30 0 0	30 0 0	do.
9 0 34	4 13 0	6 13 0	4 13 0	do.
4,433 3 35	1,499 11 0	3,631 6 4	1,464 8 6	

LEITRIM.

13 3 34	7 6 0	10 10 0	8 15 0	
19 5 13	4 15 0	6 7 10	3 16 0	
53 0 34	19 0 0	21 0 0	17 0 0	
34 0 30	13 0 0	15 10 0	11 10 0	
19 0 33	13 0 0	13 11 0	10 14 0	
16 0 33	1 0 0	5 0 0	3 13 0	
13 3 34	6 15 0	4 10 11	6 16 0	
5 3 3	5 10 0	5 13 0	3 3 0	
5 3 5	5 10 0	3 13 0	3 3 0	
22 0 33	13 7 0	10 4 10	5 0 0	
13 0 5	5 7 0	7 5 5	4 13 0	
30 3 10	unimproved	17 16 10	13 10 0	
36 1 17	15 8 0	19 0 0	14 5 0	
11 0 11	7 6 0	5 10 10	5 10 10	By agreement
11 3 0	4 0 0	7 10 10	3 10 0	

Name of Assistant Commissioners by whom Cases were decided.	No.	Name of Tenant.	Name of Landlord.	Townland.
Assistant Commissioners— D. Tuckey (Legal), R. Kenyon, S. Wilson.	5961	John Flannery,	Earl of Lucan,	Drinngar,
D. Tuckey (Legal), R. B. Hamilton, E. O'Brien.	5962	Thomas Conner, Ltd. Administrator of Ellen Conner,	Jonathan Rashleigh,	Killner,
	5964	Pat Tuvey,	do.	Kilgarriff,
	5965	Michael McGowan,	do.	do.
	5966	Patrick McGowan,	do.	do.
	5967	Thomas Heron,	do.	Derrindoorah,
	5968	Michael Reddy,	do.	do.
	5969	Mary Forkin,	do.	do.
	5970	Hugh Carney,	do.	do.
	5971	Andrew Scanlan,	Josephine G. Kennedy,	Gortdown,
	5972	Robert Curran,	Mrs. Mary Anne Hines,	Tubagh,
	5973	Patrick Conner,	Lord Harlech,	Drinagh,
	5974	Thady Tuvey,	do.	do.
	5975	John Galway, Ltd. Administrator of Edward Galway,	do.	do.
	5976	Widow Mary Rawley,	do.	do.
	5977	Michael Grady,	do.	Curranroe,
	5978	John O'Reilly,	do.	Gragacroo,
	5979	Winifred O'Neill,	do.	do.
	5980	Martin Mahoney,	do.	do.
	5981	Michael Stephens & ant.,	do.	do.
	5982	James Ragey,	Vincent Dillon,	Coolnahila,
	5983	Thomas Lynch, abscir.,	do.	Sunagh,
	5984	Bryan Gracey,	do.	Crotaree,
	5985	James Rogan,	do.	do.
	5986	Bernard O'Connor,	do.	do.
	5987	Dominick Doherty,	do.	do.
	5988	Thomas Gaughan,	do.	Knockananna,
	5989	Mary Tuvey, Ltd. Administr. of Michael Tuvey,	do.	Brownbog,
	5990	John Tuvey (Ned),	do.	do.
	5991	Pat Tuvey (Dick),	do.	do.
	5992	Pat Tuvey, senior,	do.	do.
	5993	Henry King,	do.	Derrynaslaney,
	5994	Pat Mahon (Owen),	do.	do.

MAYO.

Area of Holding. Acres.	Poor Law Valuation. £ s. d.	Former Rent. £ s. d.	Judicial Rent. £ s. d.	Observations.	Value of Tenant's £ s. d.
A. R. P.	£ s. d.	£ s. d.	£ s. d.		£ s. d.
23 3 0	5 0 0	6 10 0	5 0 0	By consent.	
15 3 7	5 0 0	6 2 0	5 3 6	With right to turbary.	
17 0 0	4 0 0	5 4 0	4 4 0	do.	
15 3 6	4 0 0	5 5 0	4 0 6	do.	
16 3 0	3 15 0	3 15 0	2 17 6	do.	
10 3 07	1 5 0	1 13 0	1 10 0	do.	
10 3 6	1 10 0	2 7 0	1 13 0	do.	
10 2 0	1 5 0	2 0 0	1 10 0	do.	
8 2 0	1 10 0	2 10 0	2 0 0	do.	
2 0 16	unascertained.	1 6 0	0 16 0		
20 0 0	4 18 6	12 1 3	10 0 6	By consent.	
13 2 15	6 0 0	7 0 0	6 14 6		
10 2 22	4 0 0	3 3 0	3 5 0		
17 0 2	5 13 0	5 0 0	4 4 0		
11 1 5	4 16 0	4 18 0	3 10 0		
20 3 25	14 5 0	11 0 0	11 0 6		
20 3 0	5 15 0	5 5 0	4 17 6		
22 0 20	5 10 0	6 0 0	4 18 0		
15 3 00	unascertained.	4 10 0	3 7 6		
42 3 10	18 0 6	17 6 6	14 15 0		
20 1 00	11 0 0	3 15 4	8 16 4		
13 0 35	5 5 0	6 15 0	3 10 6		
13 2 60	5 4 0	6 11 2	5 10 6		
11 3 16	4 15 6	5 7 8	4 6 0		
17 0 3	3 0 0	2 5 10	7 10 0		
12 3 25	9 5 0	8 13 4	8 0 6		
4 3 07	2 15 0	2 18 2	2 10 6		
22 0 15	7 4 0	2 13 0	5 5 0		
17 3 23	5 0 0	8 0 3	4 0 0		
21 1 10	11 0 0	16 15 0	6 7 4		
20 0 14	9 5 0	10 14 4	5 3 5		
10 2 30	5 5 0	7 15 0	5 15 0		
11 2 10	5 10 0	5 15 0	4 10 0		

COUNTY OF

Name of Assistant Commissioners by whom Case was decided.	No.	Name of Tenant.	Name of Landlord.	Townland.
Assistant Commissioners—				
D. Everett (Legal). R. R. Horgan. E. O'Kelly.	5895	Andrew Regan, —	Viscount Dillon, —	Cuchulard &c.,
	5896	Michael Towey (Hugh),	do. —	Cuchulard, —
	5897	James Dillon, —	Thomas Dillon, —	Behelin, —
	5898	John Garry, —	do. —	do. —
	5899	Peter Carney, —	do. —	do. —
	9000	John Duffy, —	Margaret O'Connor and minors,	Ransky, —
	9001	Thomas Leonard, Ltd. Administrator of Mary Leonard,	do. —	do. —
	9002	Michael Giblin, —	do. —	do. —
	9003	Thomas Carney, —	do. —	do. —
	9004	Martin Hopkins, —	do. —	Tumangh, —
	9005	Catherine Durry, —	do. —	Ransky, —
	9006	Mary Quin, Limited Administrator of James Quin, decd.	do. —	do. —
	9007	Patrick Hunt, —	do. —	do. —
	9008	Hugh McNulty, —	Annie J. Lyons and another, Trustees of will of Henry Lyons	Carrowmore, —
				Total,

COUNTY OF

Name of Assistant Commissioners—	No.	Name of Tenant.	Name of Landlord.	Townland.
Assistant Commissioners—				
M. T. Carran (Legal). W. J. Greehan. J. Rice.	6066	Peter Grey, ...	Michael A. Keogh and others,	Ballinrobe, —
M. T. Carran (Legal). J. MacKernan. G. S. Roberts.	6067	Patrick Flanagan,	Thos. G. W. Standford, a minor, by H. L. Jephson, his Gdn.	Clonalever, —
	6068	Bernard Green, —	do. —	Clonmell, —
	6069	William Walder, —	do. —	Clonnabunhava & another.
	6070	Michael Flynn, —	do. —	do. —
	6071	Patrick Crawley, —	do. —	Toghacom, —
	6072	Elizabeth Dillon, —	do. —	do. —
	6073	Thomas McDonough, —	do. —	do. —
	6074	Daniel Kelly, —	do. —	do. —
	6075	Michael Owen and anor.,	do. —	do. —
	6076	Patrick Lavin, —	do. —	do. —
	6077	Patrick Kelly, —	do. —	do. —
	6078	Augustin Finn, —	do. —	do. —

TABLE OF JUDICIAL RENTS.

Former Rent.	Judicial Rent.	Observations.
£ s. d.	£ s. d.	
7 13 9	6 5 0	

Name of Assistant Commissioner by whom Case was decided.	No.	Name of Tenant.	Name of Landlord.
Assistant Commissioners—			
M. T. Crean (Legal).	6079	James Finn, —	Thos. G. W. Sandford,
J. MacKinnon.	6080	Luke Flanagan, —	by H. L. Jephson, M
G. S. Boustead.	6081	John Flanagan, —	do. —
	6082	Bridget Flanagan, ..	do. —
	6083	Ann Rush, —	do. ..
	6084	Andrew Torey, —	do. —
	6085	Anne Flynn, —	do. —
	6086	Honoria Rush, —	do. —
	6087	Catherine Prendergast,	do. —
	6088	William Flanagan, ..	do. —
	6089	Patrick Finn, —	do. —
	6090	Patrick Finn (Hugh),	do. —
	6091	John Gilligan, —	do. —
	6092	Bridget Flanagan, —	do. —
	6093	Thomas Finn, —	do. —
	6094	Mary Dolan, —	do. —
	6095	Patrick Greven, —	do. —
	6096	Margaret Flynn, —	do. —
	6097	Dominick Flanagan, —	do. —
	6098	Michael Hanly, —	do. —
	6099	Michael Flanagan, —	do. —
	6100	Thomas Flanagan, ..	do. —
	6101	Mary Mahon, —	do. —

ROSCOMMON—continued.

Amount of Holding.	Poor Law Valuation.	Former Rent.	Judicial Rent.	Observations.
A. R. P.	£ s. d.	£ s. d.	£ s. d.	
19 8 20	5 0 0	8 15 0	4 5 0	
21 1 0	4 15 0	4 15 0	1 0 0	
13 2 0	1 17 0	2 11 0	5 0 0	
14 3 0	6 0 0	6 15 6	5 10 0	
11 8 20	5 5 0	8 7 6	5 0 0	
12 2 00	8 10 6	11 8 0	8 10 8	
24 0 10	8 10 6	12 3 0	9 0 0	
21 1 80	2 15 0	4 5 0	5 15 0	
13 0 0	5 15 0	5 15 9	4 0 0	
8 1 20	3 5 0	6 0 0	5 10 0	
16 3 20	4 10 0	8 5 0	4 0 0	
21 1 20	4 5 0	6 1 0	9 15 0	
10 3 0	1 5 0	9 5 0	1 10 0	
16 0 10	2 10 0	3 10 0	8 0 0	
18 1 10	2 10 0	1 15 0	3 16 0	
14 5 25	4 10 0	5 15 0	6 0 0	
19 3 0	5 15 0	6 12 6	6 5 0	
20 8 16	7 5 0	10 11 0	7 0 8	
14 3 20	8 0 0	7 10 8	5 0 0	
14 0 20	0 15 0	1 10 0	1 10 0	
22 2 20	5 10 0	7 9 6	5 0 0	
6 6 20	4 15 0	5 0 0	3 7 0	
9 5 20	6 10 0	5 0 0	2 15 0	
18 2 10	5 0 0	4 4 0	9 5 0	
17 1 30	6 15 0	5 6 8	4 0 0	
16 5 10	4 15 0	5 6 0	6 14 0	
4 5 20	9 5 0	2 13 3	1 15 0	
8 3 20	5 6 0	3 5 6	2 10 0	
14 0 0	5 10 0	1 16 0	3 10 0	
12 2 20	8 5 0	5 15 5	4 6 6	
10 1 20	8 15 0	5 15 1	5 10 0	
11 1 20	7 10 0	8 6 6	6 6 0	
10 2 0	8 5 0	2 10 0	3 15 0	
30 3 0	8 15 0	6 6 0	2 17 0	
14 3 20	7 10 0	9 0 0	6 10 0	

Town of Address, Commissioners by whom Cases were decided.	No.	Name of Tenant.	Name of Landlord.	Townland.
Assistant Commissioners—				
M. E. Green (Legal).	6114	Dominick Flanagan,	Thos. C. W. Sandford, assigns	Cloonduavee,
J. MacKenna,			by H. L. Jephson, his Com.	
O. S. Foster	6115	Patrick Flanagan, Ltd. Administrator Flanagan.	do.	do.
	6116	Bridget Levin,	do.	do.
	6117	Patrick Levin,	do.	do.
	6118	Thomas Quinn,	do.	do.
	6119	John Gaynor and anor.	do.	Cloncolt,
	6120	Patrick Rafferty,	do.	do.
	6121	John Smith,	do.	do.
	6122	Patrick Kelly, Rep. of William Kelly.	do.	do.
	6123	Bernard Gowla,	do.	do.
	6124	Thomas Egan,	do.	do.
	6125	Honor Mulholland (John) and another.	do.	Tephanan,
	6126	Roger Doherty,	do.	Clonsilloran,
	6127	Patrick Flynn and anor.	do.	Tagharean,
	6128	Peter McDermott,	do.	do.
	6129	Dominick Flanagan and another.	do.	do.
	6130	Patrick Flanagan,	do.	do.
	6131	Michael McDermott junior.	do.	do.
	6132	Michael Byrne,	do.	do.
	6133	Mark Flanagan,	do.	do.
	6134	Bernard McDermott,	do.	do.
	6135	Anna Byrne,	do.	do.
	6136	John Kelly,	do.	do.
	6137	Mary Flannin,	do.	do.
	6138	John Flanagan,	do.	do.
	6139	Thomas Callaghan,	do.	do.
	6140	William White,	do.	do.
	6141	Nicholas White,	do.	do.
	6142	Mary Fleming,	do.	do.
	6143	Thomas Doolinery,	do.	Clooneen
	6144	James Croke,	do.	Daghearra,
	6145	Michael Birney,	do.	Clonetowin
	6146	Thomas Crawley,	do.	do.
	6147	Patrick Crawley,	do.	do.
	6148	Peter Levin,	do.	do.

Printed copies obtained by the Librarian of Representative Church Body, Dublin from OPR

ROSCOMMON—*continued*

Extent of Holding Statute	Poor Law Valuation	Present Rent	Judicial Rent	Observations	Value of Tenancy
a. r. p.	£ s. d.	£ s. d.	£ s. d.		£ s. d.
57 1 30	7 5 0	10 12 0	8 7 0		
13 0 10	1 18 0	7 4 0	1 18 0		
11 0 0	6 0 0	6 10 0	4 7 0		
12 8 10	4 5 0	4 5 0	4 10 0		
11 2 30	4 0 0	5 14 0	4 0 0		
7 3 30	8 10 0	4 15 0	5 5 0		
9 0 15	3 5 0	3 9 0	2 18 0		
14 1 30	2 0 0	2 14 0	2 3 0		
12 3 0	2 15 0	8 14 0	8 5 0		
9 1 15	3 0 0	3 10 10	4 0 0		
14 0 0	6 10 0	8 19 9	6 0 0		
10 3 30	5 5 0	5 0 0	3 9 0		
17 1 30	3 0 0	5 6 0	4 8 0		
15 0 30	5 15 0	6 17 6	6 18 0		
13 0 0	8 15 0	5 0 0	8 5 0		
18 1 0	0 5 0	6 15 6	4 5 0		
18 0 0	4 10 6	5 5 0	3 15 0		
13 8 0	8 15 0	4 5 0	2 0 0		
9 0 0	3 0 0	4 10 0	2 3 0		
28 0 0	5 5 0	7 7 6	8 10 0		
8 1 0	3 10 0	4 17 0	3 5 0		
10 1 0	4 5 0	5 8 6	9 4 0		
11 0 30	8 0 0	3 8 6	3 10 0		
15 3 0	2 15 0	3 14 0	3 0 0		
25 3 0	6 15 6	8 15 0	6 10 0		
13 8 10	5 10 0	9 15 9	5 0 0		
11 0 0	8 0 0	6 2 6	8 10 0		
8 0 0	3 5 0	3 15 0	2 10 0		
17 8 30	5 13 0	7 0 0	4 17 0		
15 0 0	2 10 0	1 10 0	1 0 0		
19 0 0	4 5 0	5 0 0	3 8 0		
18 2 30	1 7 0	8 1 0	1 7 0		
14 0 5	8 10 0	9 18 6	5 0 0		
33 0 5	7 6 8	9 0 0	7 10 0		
17 1 0	7 15 0	10 16 0	4 6 0		

Name of Assistant Commissioners by whom Cases were decided.	No.	Name of Tenant.	Name of Landlord.
Assistant Commissioners—			
M. T. Cullen (Legal).	6149	Francis Green, —	Thos. G. W. Sandford
J. MacKenzie.			by H. L. Jephson,
G. S. Bolster.	6150	Mary Green (John), —	do. —

ROSCOMMON—*continued.*

Extent of Holdings. Acres.	Poor Law Valuation.	Former Rent.	Judicial Rent.	Observations.
A. R. P.	£ s. d.	£ s. d.	£ s. d.	
15 3 0	3 5 0	3 5 0	3 5 0	
17 3 0	4 0 0	4 4 4	3 7 0	
3 1 0	2 0 0	2 14 0	2 0 0	
15 0 20	5 10 0	6 5 0	4 10 0	
6 3 20	3 5 0	5 13 5	2 7 0	
15 2 0	6 5 0	7 6 0	5 5 0	
10 3 18	2 15 0	3 14 6	5 0 0	
13 2 10	3 10 0	4 10 0	3 5 0	
13 2 0	2 5 0	3 3 0	2 10 0	
31 1 85	7 0 0	6 14 0	7 10 0	
18 0 0	7 5 0	6 16 4	5 0 0	
13 1 0	3 0 0	5 1 4	2 15 0	
1,418 0 35	434 15 6	522 0 6	373 2 4	

SLIGO.

6 1 5	9 10 0	5 13 6	2 5 0	
16 6 0	5 5 0	6 16 5	6 14 2	
4 1 0	7 15 0	9 0 0	5 0 0	
38 0 24	19 10 0	17 6 0	17 8 6	
24 1 8	15 10 0	21 0 6	13 10 6	
14 1 30	10 5 0	11 3 6	10 0 0	
9 3 31	6 5 0	9 0 0	7 18 0	
3 0 0	5 15 0	5 10 0	3 5 0	
25 0 0	18 0 0	18 8 0	15 0 0	
72 3 15	23 5 0	34 0 0	25 0 0	
37 2 5	22 15 0	24 5 5	23 0 0	
7 1 5	16 0 0	18 0 0	13 0 0	
31 1 7	16 10 0	16 19 5	18 19 5	
13 2 31	8 0 0	8 14 6	8 10 0	
9 0 14	5 5 0	5 10 0	4 0 0	
13 0 0	8 11 0	10 10 0	8 15 0	

Names of Assistant Commissioners by whom Cases were Decided.	No.	Name of Tenant.	Name of Landlord.	Townland.
Assistant Commissioners:— D. Tuohy (Legal). R. Sproule. S. Willey.	4736	Patrick Toomey, Limtd. Admor. of Sarah Toomey	Myles H. Cregan,	Ardmackan,
	4737	William Fisher,	do.	do.
	4738	James Mahony,	do.	do.
	4739	Patrick Flannery,	do.	do.
	4740	Michael Carey, surgeon,	do.	do.
	4741	Margaret Kenny, Limtd. Admrx. of John Kenny,	Farrell Cunihan and another,	Dromduhheen,
	4742	Mary Frawley,	do.	do.
	4743	Timothy Wynne, custd. in name of Thomas Kevil	do.	do.
	4744	Thomas McDarmott,	Sir Gilbert King, Bart.	Whitehill,
	4745	Pat Sweeny,	do.	do.
	4746	Owen McDermott,	do.	Carrowbane,
	4747	John O'Hara,	do.	do.
	4748	Patrick McDermott,	do.	Oughers,
	4749	Jacob Martin,	do.	Oughers and etc.
	4750	James Mulholland,	do.	do.
	4751	Thomas Cooke, Limtd. Admor. of Martin Downes	Colonel E. H. Cooper,	Knockbeg,
	4752	Michael Spillane,	do.	Carrowkelly,
	4753	Patty Brennan,	do.	do.
	4754	Margaret Kerrigan,	do.	Cashlen,
	4755	John Judge,	do.	Killola,
	4756	Henry Whitmell, junior,	do.	Derrees,
	4757	Do.	do.	do.
	4758	Henry Whitmell, senior,	do.	Derryhal and etc.
	4759	Alexander Reed,	do.	Tullynoory,
	4760	Robert Williams, Limtd. Admor. of James Graham,	do.	Ballygawley,
	4761	Mrs. Kate Weald,	do.	do.
	4762	Margaret Kelly,	do.	do.
	4763	Robert Williams, Limtd. Admor. of James Graham,	do.	Dromahair,
	4764	James Kelly,	do.	Kasheen,

Report of Holding Bounds	Poor Law Valuation			Former Rent			Judicial Rent		
A. R. P.	£	s.	d.	£	s.	d.	£	s.	d.
2 1 23	5	0	0	10	0	0	5	15	0
3 0 15	3	0	0	6	10	0	2	10	0
11 1 29	unascertained,			11	1	5	7	3	0
15 1 03	13	5	0	13	10	0	11	5	0
17 0 33	10	10	0	13	0	0	10	5	0
11 3 15	7	0	0	6	5	0	6	0	0
57 0 7	unascertained,			33	0	0	23	0	0
10 0 36	6	0	0	5	0	0	5	10	0
63 3 23	47	10	0	44	15	6	35	10	0
15 3 30	10	5	0	10	15	7	8	5	0
25 0 36	8	15	0	8	13	3	9	10	0
13 3 0	13	0	0	13	3	4	10	10	0
4 3 0	5	5	0	3	15	3	3	0	0
17 0 36	10	15	0	13	15	10	9	15	0
10 2 13	5	5	0	5	0	0	4	15	0
17 3 3	63	0	0	55	0	0	15	15	0
34 0 30	15	10	0	19	11	0	14	5	0
35 3 13	15	0	0	19	5	0	13	15	0
54 3 0	61	5	0	55	0	0	45	10	0
30 1 36	11	5	0	16	0	0	10	5	0
34 0 5	25	5	0	57	0	0	17	0	0
16 0 31	10	10	0	11	5	0	8	0	0
53 3 11	54	5	0	55	10	0	45	0	0
30 1 30	19	15	0	20	0	0	17	10	0
7 3 15	6	15	0	7	0	0	5	10	0
13 3 15	14	5	0	15	0	0	10	0	0
15 3 33	7	10	0	7	0	0	5	5	0
43 3 23	35	5	0	56	0	0	27	0	0
31 3 44	5	0	0	5	0	0	6	10	0
63 3 0	19	5	0	17	3	0	46	0	0
10 3 36	8	0	0	10	0	0	6	10	0
63 3 33	14	15	0	15	0	0	15	15	0
15 0 35	8	15	0	7	15	6	7	0	0
11 5 30	14	5	0	17	5	3	12	5	3

Name of Assistant Commissioners by whom Case was decided	No.	Name of Tenant.	Name of Landlord.	Townland.
Assistant Commissioners—				
D. Tighe (Legal), R. Stirling, R. Munson.	4770	Michael Devanny,	Earl of Erne,	Carrowkeel,
	4771	Michael Scanlon,	do.	do.
	4772	John Devanny,	do.	do.
	4773	James Devanny,	do.	Carrowmore,
	4774	Thomas Gryan,	do.	do.
	4775	William Scanlon,	do.	do.
	4776	James Tim,	do.	do.
	4777	Widow Mary Keighan and another,	do.	Brenagan,
	4778	Michael Brew,	do.	do.
	4779	Hugh Harte,	do.	do.
	4780	Michael O'Gun,	do.	Graigue, North,
	4781	James Reaney,	do.	do.
	4782	Owen Brennan, enttd. in name of B. Brennan,	do.	do.
	4783	John Hart,	do.	Knockmoyer, Sth.
	4784	Pat Sweeny,	do.	do.
				Total,

PROVINCE OF

Assistant Commissioners—				
J. S. Green, q.c. (Legal), J. Martin, J. Gilmaine.	5301	Ellen Brew,	W. C. V. Barton,	Moyaddamore,
J. S. Green, q.c (Legal), W. S. Hunt, H. C. Nash.	5302	James Hogan,	Lord Dunboyne,	Ballyvaness,
	5303	John McInerney,	Lord Lanesfield,	Garrnaboy,
	5304	James Mahony,	John Scanlan and others,	Ballyskenagan,
				Total,

SLIGO—continued

Contents of Holdings.	Poor Law Valuation.	Former Rent.	Judicial Rent.	Observations.
A. R. P.	£ s. d.	£ s. d.	£ s. d.	
10 3 30	7 15 0	7 7 0	6 15 0	
21 3 37	14 15 0	14 5 8	10 0 0	
6 0 30	6 10 0	5 15 8	4 10 0	
10 0 5	8 0 0	9 1 8	8 0 0	
13 3 23	8 15 0	11 6 0	8 0 0	
16 3 0	11 5 0	18 10 0	10 15 0	
9 1 33	6 5 0	7 3 0	6 15 0	
23 3 14	17 10 0	18 15 0	13 15 0	
9 1 10	7 15 0	9 8 0	6 10 0	
6 0 0	5 10 0	6 7 8	4 13 0	And an undivided ¼ of 16 A. 20 r.
23 1 33	11 5 0	14 10 0	13 10 0	
7 0 15	4 15 0	5 4 0	4 5 0	
15 0 30	9 10 0	8 15 0	7 0 0	
16 3 30	13 0 0	11 10 0	9 5 0	
13 6 13	13 10 0	11 0 0	6 10 0	
1,001 0 54	899 10 0	1,000 14 4	778 1 8	

MUNSTER.

	No.	Name of Tenant.	Name of Landlord.	Parish.
HALF COMMISSION.	5844	Margaret Crowley,	Very Rev. H. Fleming,	Rathmullogy,
Assistant Commissioners—	4944	Hugh Kelleher,	Henry O. Warren,	Cullackingroe,
L. DOYLE (Legal).	5945	Denis Keefe,	Jeremiah Hegarty,	Castellner,
R. R. BAYLY.	5947	Thomas Mulhern,	William H. H. Massy,	Ballintin,
R. W. CRADDOCK.	5948	Cornelius Moynihan,	Michael Kelleher,	Kilkeedy,
	5949	Jeremiah Singleton,	H. C. Newman,	Rath-Knock,
	5950	William Flinn,	Francis W. Low and others,	Clavaghan,
	5951	John Lyon,	James Moriarty and others, Estate of John Moriarty,	Kilmanin,
	5952	Michael Lynch,	do.	do.
	5955	Austin White,	Mrs. Jane J. Simpson,	Balldahan,
	5955	Timothy Sullivan,	Henry A. E. Wills,	Drommaditto,
	5956	Do.	do.	do.
	5956	Ellen Buckley,	do.	Shehina,
	5957	James Quinlan,	E. O. Nunan,	Barrin,
L. DOYLE (Legal).	5958	Michael Madden,	James Grant,	Loslin Chort,
J. J. GUIRE.	5959	James Sheeton,	George Eborall,	Derrynlieve,
M. KELLY.	5960	Denis Regan,	Mark Cahill and others,	Derig,
	5961	Samuel Kingston,	do.	Tullig,
	5962	Ellen Donovan and sisters,	do.	do.
	5963	Richard L. Aldman and sisters,	Munster and Leinster Bank,	Monevan,
	5964	Joseph Sheehan,	Very Rev. H. T. Fleming and others,	Monagrees and others,
	5965	John Callaghan,	James Baldwin,	do.
	5966	Jeremiah Mahony,	James G. Oswald,	Blankmarsh,
	5967	Owen Fitzgerald,	Captain Theobld Connor,	Gerrinabigh,
	5968	Anne Callaghan,	Rev. George Blacklck,	Bellowen,
	5969	William Wells,	Bampiny T. Brandish, a minor, by Hannah Renwick, Administratrix,	Cloghgh,
	5970	Michael Guilnane,	do.	Kllanicoola,
	5971	John Doggan,	Reginald B. Jones,	Castellsby,
	5972	William S. Peterson,	George Staunton, a lunatic, by Simpson Staunell and another, his Committee.	Drommagarbh,

With undivided moiety of grazing on 2½ acres and six [illegible] of [illegible] Mountain.

Name of Assistant Commissioners by whom Cases were decided.	No.	Name of Tenant.	Name of Landlord.	Townland.
Assistant Commissioners— L. DOYLE (Legal). F. J. GUINY. M. HEALY.	6073	Daniel Deasy,	Amos Galloway and another,	Dunbeady,
	6074	John Collinson,	Lord Carbery,	Oakaring,
	6075	James Fielding,	Mathew O'Flea and another,	Knuginobin,
	6076	Patrick Keohane,	Captain John Allen,	Donaloody,
	6077	Timothy T. Heyet,	Lord Carbery,	Cragg,
	6078	Denis Gallagher,	Mrs. A. M. Campbell,	Barley Hill,
	6079	Timothy Fitzpatrick, Ltd. Admor. of Daniel Fitzpatrick,	John H. Townsend, served to nomme of Richard H. Townsend,	Knockfune,
	5688	James Minnole,	do.	Seen,
	5681	Thomas Hogan,	do.	do.
	6282	Timothy Bickey,	do.	Banminneninin,
	6083	Patrick Regen,	James Beamish,	Careiptiolde,
	6084	John Donovan,	do.	do.
	5685	John Deacon,	do.	Corrigeounane,
	5682	Richard Fitzpatrick,	James McCarthy,	Benlad,
L. DOYLE (Legal). W. WALPOLE. O. VANBRETH.	5987	John Sullivan,	Thomas Gilbman,	Crooang,
	5988	James Creein,	do.	do.
	5989	William Costin,	Mrs. Kate O'Sullivan,	Beendyancer,
	5990	James Whensson,	Robert H. R. Walns,	Boualt,
	4291	John Spillane,	Rev. John Clerke,	Bublenn,
	5622	Robert Werner, junior,	Earl of Bantry,	Spoonbegurk,
	5643	Julia Coghlan,	William Bird and another,	Townoursork,

CORK—*continued.*

Extent of Holding Acres.	Poor Law Valuation.	Former Rent.	Judicial Rent.	Observations.
A. R. P.	£ s. d.	£ s. d.	£ s. d.	
38 3 28	19 15 0	27 16 5	19 10 0	
10 0 0	8 5 0	7 10 0	5 17 6	
8 3 20	6 15 0	6 0 0	5 6 0	
19 6 27	16 10 0	16 0 0	14 13 5	
38 1 57	6 5 0	13 0 0	10 5 0	
29 0 0	18 0 8	27 10 0	17 7 6	
29 1 7	9 5 0	7 5 0	6 5 0	
60 2 0	31 10 0	38 0 0	31 0 0	
121 3 1	54 15 0	69 0 0	51 5 0	
39 1 7	10 10 0	11 15 0	9 10 0	
18 0 0	6 5 0	5 0 0	5 10 0	
45 0 0	21 5 0	31 0 0	12 10 0	
154 0 31	35 5 0	41 0 0	34 0 0	
1 0 0	unascertained	5 0 0	3 0 0	
—				
631 1 5	30 10 0	48 0 0	30 0 0	
511 3 5	17 0 0	28 0 0	20 0 0	
163 1 20	43 10 0	56 0 0	44 0 0	
16 0 0	38 10 0	40 0 0	28 0 0	
39 3 31	6 15 0	7 10 0	6 0 0	With right of grazing on mountain.
36 3 13	34 15 0	33 0 0	36 10 0	
18 0 5	9 5 0	12 0 0	6 5 0	With ⅓ undivided of 172A. 1 R. 14 P. mountain grazing.
17 1 50	6 0 0	5 0 0	5 0 0	With ½ undivided of 36 acres.
13 3 19	6 5 0	11 14 0	5 0 0	
30 0 0	5 10 0	10 0 0	7 5 0	
40 0 0	12 10 0	14 0 0	10 0 0	With right of grazing on Gonelamore Mountain.
31 0 0	10 0 0	12 0 0	9 10 0	
91 0 0	17 10 0	19 15 0	18 0 0	
43 1 15	20 5 0	21 5 8	17 7 6	
37 1 18	6 15 0	18 13 4	8 0 0	
3 3 5	2 10 0	3 13 9	3 10 0	
45 3 0	14 0 0	15 10 6	12 0 0	With right of grazing on Grotinus

Assistant Commissioners—

L. Doyle (Legal).
W. Walpole.
O. Vansittart.

6004	Denis F. Shea,	...	Lord O. F. F. Clinton,	
6005	Patrick Sidley,	...	do.	...
6006	Michael Harrington,	...	do.	...
6007	Patrick Sullivan,	...	do.	...
6008	Timothy Sullivan,	...	do.	...
6009	Daniel Curry,	...	do.	...

CORK—continued.

Extent of Holding. Statute.	Poor-Law Valuation.	Former Rent.	Judicial Rent.	Observations.
A. R. P.	£ s. d.	£ s. d.	£ s. d.	
14 0 32	5 2 0	5 15 6	4 5 0	With right of grazing on Muddle Mountains with 23 others.
7 3 33	5 0 0	6 15 6	5 10 0	
34 0 10	30 4 0	27 10 0	20 0 0	With right of grazing on Ballingeary Mountains in common with other tenants.
1 3 0	4 13 0	7 3 0	3 3 0	With right of grazing on Derryvacurra Mountain with other tenants.
17 3 26	6 10 0	5 5 0	4 13 0	With right of grazing on Clondrohid Mountain.
34 3 0	4 19 0	5 0 0	4 0 0	With right of grazing on Muddle Mountain in common with 25 others.
4 2 3	9 19 0	5 0 0	2 3 6	do.
23 3 10	9 15 0	10 7 0	9 0 0	do.
18 3 5	5 0 0	4 17 4	4 0 0	do.
13 3 0	3 17 0	4 0 0	3 0 0	do.
8 0 5	4 7 5	3 3 0	2 10 0	do.
3 3 30	0 13 0	3 0 0	1 10 0	With right of grazing on Hungry Hill.
10 1 30	7 0 0	7 15 3	6 0 0	With right of grazing on Mizen Mountain.
12 1 22	4 0 0	6 0 0	4 0 0	With right of grazing on Kilcrowea Mountain.
16 3 10	3 3 0	5 0 0	3 2 0	With right of grazing on Drumgariff Mountain.
13 3 30	4 5 0	5 0 0	6 0 0	do.
28 0 27	5 3 0	3 13 0	3 0 0	With right of grazing on Derry-lough Mountain.
31 2 30	49 15 0	120 0 0	93 0 0	By consent.
30 0 0	76 0 0	113 6 0	84 0 0	do.
13 3 0	7 0 0	10 0 0	7 0 0	do.
13 0 0	7 13 0	10 0 0	7 16 0	do.
14 0 0	7 0 0	9 10 0	7 0 0	do.
11 3 36	10 5 0	14 8 10	12 10 0	
3,553 0 1	1,347 5 0	1,806 11 0	1,378 13 0	

Names of Assistant Commissioners by whom Cases were decided.	No.	Name of Tenant.	Name of Landlord.	Townland.
Assistant Commissioners— J. R. Green, &c. (Legal). H. C. Grasby. W. H. Brewster.	2425	Michael O'Shaughnessy	Miss Frances Reyne and another.	Corrabhanna
	2426	James Morgan	The James Folle	Ballygolistion & another
	2427	James Madigan	Mrs. Mary Schreiburg	Shanagolden Demesne
	2428	James O'Connor	La Morshess Dolls Brooks	Drummorlan
	2429	Catharine McCoy	do.	Doonaha
	2430	Ellen Hinley	do.	do.
	2431	Brenda Fitzgerald	Knight of Glin	Ballygubtown, E.
	2432	Bridget Fenton	do.	Cahernrigh
	2433	John Ahaurn	do.	do.
				Total,

Assistant Commissioners— J. H. Lynn (Legal). L. Carney. R. H. Patrick.	3697	Mary Grace, Limited Ad. of John Grace	William Byrne, continued in name of C. A. Byrne.	Killbyne
	3698	Patrick Sheas	George O'Brien	Garrykennedy
	3699	Patrick Gleeson	do.	do.
	3700	John Winde	William Speight, continued in name of Sir James Speight.	Derrybeg and another
	3701	John Loughrane	Robert Rea	Nantanagh
	3702	Patrick Grace	do.	
	3703	Thomas Ryan	do.	Oprellan
	3704	William Ryan	do.	do.
	3705	Dan Maher	George A. Mullin	Borrisoge
	3706	John Kennedy	Richard Lloyd	Killough
	3707	Bridget Hampleton	do.	do.
	3708	Margaret Stephenson	do.	Cloonada
	3709	Daniel Fogarty	do.	do.
	3710	William Maher	do.	do.
	3711	James Ryan	do.	do.
	3712	John Meehan	do.	do.
	3713	Martin Treacy	do.	Clonboo
	3714	John Hamblin	do.	Killough
	3715	James Ryan	P.F.	do.

Name of Assistant Commissioners by whom Case was decided.	No.	Name of Tenant.	Name of Landlord.	Townland.
J. R. Stone (Legal) L. Connor, H. H. Finnick.	3717	Martin Hickie,	Henry J. Lloyd,	Ellistrudy,
	3718	Thomas Hickie,	do.	do.
	3719	James Davis,	do.	do.
	3720	Patrick Halloran,	do.	do.
	3721	William Keough,	do.	do.
	3722	Philip Hoban,	do.	do.
	3723	Margaret Hoban,	do.	do.
	3724	Thomas Farnwell,	Miss Philly Fairfield,	Claremore,
	3725	Patrick Hynes,	Michael Gallaghan,	Brusha,
	3726	William O'Meara, raised in trust of Jas. Haugh,	George Bixton,	Arvagh,
	3727	John A. Carden,	do.	do.
	3728	Patrick Hogan,	W. D. Pepper,	Kilira,
	3729	John Lawlor,	do.	Slaugh,
	3730	James Devitt,	do.	Kilfinane,
	3731	William Hogan,	do.	do.
	3732	Julia Fitzgerald, Limited Admin. of Michael Fitzgerald,	Mrs. Sarah Sheppard,	Ballingarry,
	3733	Fernando Martin,	do.	do.
	3734	Thomas Haugh,	do.	do.
	3735	Margaret Cleary,	do.	do.
	3736	Thomas Caissher,	James Esqueda,	Dooanstongh,
	3737	Francres Talbot,	Lady Mary Morris,	Curramwork and additional.
	3738	George F. Kent,	Colonel James F. Blakey,	Killeen,
	3739	Patrick Dolan,	William F. H. L. Vaughan,	Ballylieg,
	3740	Michael Banbury,	Miss Catherine Lloyd,	Cardihere,
J. R. Enes (Legal) F. M. Carroll, E. G. Pere.	3741	Thomas Quinnane,	Lieutenant John G. Packer,	Cotleen,
	3742	William Early (William),	George B. M. Dawnes,	Longford,
	3743	John Haynes,	Frederick Kennedy,	Sheleen,
	3744	James Lawlor,	Miss Mary Going,	Ballydavth,
	3745	Mary Sullivan,	do.	do.

TIPPERARY—*continued.*

Amount of Holding—Acres.	Poor Law Valuation.	Former Rent.	Judicial Rent.	Observations.	Value of Tenancy.
A. R. P.	£ s. d.	£ s. d.	£ s. d.		£ s. d.
12 1 21	22 18 0	22 10 0	18 15 0		
16 3 29	10 5 0	14 5 0	13 14 0		
19 2 10	18 0 0	10 15 0	10 15 0		
47 0 27	29 10 0	54 10 0	37 0 0		
81 1 19	22 5 8	61 9 11	28 12 0		
28 1 6	unascertained,	29 0 0	31 5 0		
27 3 21	do.	23 15 0	25 10 0		
25 0 12	16 3 0	13 6 0	11 14 0		
8 0 0	unascertained,	1 8 10	1 8 10		
127 0 21	43 15 0	44 10 0	49 14 0		
43 8 68	21 0 0	34 5 0	32 3 10		
11 3 30	4 10 0	8 19 0	3 17 0		
99 8 3	45 0 0	30 0 0	30 0 0		
44 0 10	23 10 0	23 4 10	30 1 0		
21 1 21	11 5 0	11 11 5	8 11 0		
4 8 28	2 10 0	2 18 6	2 16 8		
6 3 5	2 10 0	6 2 8	3 10 0		
5 0 0	3 3 0	3 16 4	2 11 0		
17 8 18	9 6 0	14 6 0	11 18 0		
20 5 8	unascertained,	16 0 0	13 15 0		
43 5 29	25 15 0	88 10 4	13 10 3		
32 3 17	26 6 0	41 15 8	42 17 0		
10 2 10	6 0 0	6 0 0	8 5 0		
48 3 5	30 5 0	15 0 0	24 12 0		
21 1 22	11 11 0	16 15 0	11 0 0	By consent.	
6 2 0	3 0 0	4 0 0	3 0 0	do.	
57 3 55	31 10 0	33 3 0	57 5 0	.	
29 0 13	14 10 0	31 19 6	16 0 0		
15 1 57	7 5 0	20 15 0	13 0 0		
29 1 16	13 0 0	18 0 0	13 0 0		
57 8 88	24 10 0	31 10 6	31 10 0		
70 8 13	56 10 0	71 1 7	58 0 0		

72

IRISH LAND COMMISSION.

COUNTY OF

Name of Assistant Commissioners by whom Cases were decided	No.	Name of Tenant	Name of Landlord	Townland
Assistant Commissioners—				
J. H. KERR (Legal).	5749	Thomas Russell,	George F. Lalor,	Barnakilmore,
F. M. CARROLL.	5750	William Dwyer,	do.	Derryville,
R. G. PEW.	5751	Mary Russell,	do.	Longorchard,
	5752	Thomas Lloyd,	Charles Lloyd,	Lisheen,
	5753	Daniel Brahm,	Captain Evelyn Lloyd,	Cranagh,
	5754	John Quinnee,	Mrs. Anne Hanly,	Finlly,
	5755	Maurice McGrath,	Captain Edward Armstrong,	Moynith,
	5756	Allen Costello,	do.	do.
	5757	Judith Dwyer,	do.	do.
	5758	Michael Kennedy,	Commissioners of National Schools in Ireland,	Limerore,
	5759	Patrick Fanning,	John Fennelly,	Gustnorra,
	5760	Bridget Quinlan,	do.	do.
	5761	Daniel Healy,	Provost, &c., of Trinity College, Dublin,	College Hill,
	5762	Edmund Fogarty,	Sir John G. Carden, Bart.,	Lissavirdoge,
	5763	Honoria Ryan,	Major Butler Kearney,	Drum,
	5764	John Ryan,	do.	do.
	5765	John Kavanagh,	Henry J. Lloyd,	Knocke,
	5766	Michael Ryan,	John Bennett, a minor, by Florence Bennett, his Gdn.	Killaserrie,
	5767	John Ryan (Martin),	Miss Grace Cooke,	Garryngrona,
	5768	James Fogarty,	do.	do.
	5769	Edmund Quinlan,	do.	Garryngrona, Up.
				Total,

COUNTY OF

Assistant Commissioners—	1353	Michael Power,	Ellen Gordon,	Kumbicon,
J. S. OXLEY, Q.C. (Legal).	1348	John O'Meara,	James F. Molony,	Lower Servilton,
J. HAUNTON.	1341	Catherine Divan,	Count de la Poer,	Tantinarra,
J. J. O'SHAUGHNESSY.	1349	William Houlahan,	do.	Glen, Upper,
	1845	Catherine Moore,	Lord Ashtown,	Curraghtaskin,
				Total,

TIPPERARY—*continued*

Extent of Holding. Acres.	Poor Law Valuation.	Former Rent.	Judicial Rent.	Observations.
A. R. P.	£ s. d.	£ s. d.	£ s. d.	
83 3 18	39 5 0	33 12 1½	24 0 0	
128 3 17	54 4 0	70 0 0	54 0 0	
33 3 8	27 10 0	25 6 5	21 10 0	
6 2 0	5 5 0	3 10 0	3 10 0	
4 3 1	4 0 0	5 0 0	7 10 0	
37 1 1	not ascertained,	13 13 9	13 13 9	
28 0 14	do.	19 10 0	20 10 0	
6 2 14	8 18 0	8 10 0	5 0 0	
23 2 5	31 2 0	53 4 0	19 0 0	
44 3 9	34 15 0	34 17 5	30 0 0	
41 2 12	20 0 0	28 0 0	19 0 0	
39 1 0	17 10 0	14 6 5	15 10 0	
6 3 27	6 0 0	5 6 0	4 0 0	
93 3 27	105 0 0	110 2 5	100 0 0	
47 0 25	46 5 0	47 10 0	33 6 0	
42 1 5	39 10 0	48 10 0	34 0 0	
3 3 12	2 15 0	6 19 5	3 5 0	
18 0 23	13 5 0	16 6 0	10 0 0	
14 0 31	7 0 0	9 17 4	6 0 0	
8 3 7	7 5 0	13 7 6	10 0 0	
13 1 9	5 0 0	8 5 7	6 10 0	
2,476 3 23	1,364 15 0	1,716 17 3½	1,290 13 6	

WATERFORD.

CIVIL BILL

PROVINCE OF

COUNTY OF

Name of Tenant.	Name of Landlord.	Townland.
...t Lemke, Rep. of ...trick Green,	H. N. Thorpe and another,	Curtin, ...
...s Proctor, ...	Rev. George Lewis and others,	Kavama, ...
...ams Friself, ...	do.	do. ...
...s Robinson, ...	F. R. Guru, a lunatic, by Cecilia F. Thorpe and anor., his Committee.	Garagh, ...
Do.	do.	Duvycuw, ...
Do., ...	do.	do. ...
...s Saunderson and ors.	do.	Givanna, ...
		Total. ...

COUNTY OF

COURTS.

ULSTER.

ARMAGH.

Extent of Holding. Quant.	Poor Law Valuation.	Former Rent.	Judicial Rent.	Observations.	Value of Tenancy.
A. R. P.	£ s. d.	£ s. d.	£ s. d.		£ s. d.
13 1 34	4 5 0	6 0 0	4 17 0		
5 1 15	5 15 0	5 13 5	4 0 0		
16 1 20	23 0 0	19 11 9	15 13 0		
3 0 21	unascertained,	1 15 8	1 3 6		
1 3 16	do.	2 5 6	1 12 0		
5 0 16	do.	7 10 0	6 0 0		
73 0 23	34 0 0	31 5 7	13 0 0		
67 1 32	63 0 0	73 16 1	53 4 6		

CAVAN.

23 0 34	10 5 0	9 10 0	6 5 8		
25 0 0	6 0 0	7 19 0	5 0 0		
13 0 0	7 0 0	6 3 0	4 5 0	By consent.	
10 1 1	6 5 0	8 2 5	3 3 5	do.	
1 5 9	3 0 0	3 15 3	2 10 0		
15 0 14	7 10 0	8 0 0	5 5 0		

CIVIL BILL COURTS.

COUNTY OF

Name of Tenant.	Name of Landlord.	Townland.
Edward Brady,	Colonel James Graham and another, Exors. of Daniel Callinara.	Gartabragh,
James King,	Hugh Grehan,	Drumallien,
Thomas McGovern,	Rev. Frederick Elliott,	Danghra,
Edward Brady,	G. J. Topham,	Lisbi,
Owen Clarke,	Lady Garvagh,	Carmaveaham,
Thomas Mawnton,	William A. Rogers,	Dramhed,
John White,	Hugh O'Reilly and another,	Derrelars,
Owen Cusack,	Sophia Crawford,	Lisstream,
James Carroll,	Robert Morgan and another,	Monaghamann,
Thomas F. McCabe,	George Clarke,	Corrgh Glebe,
John McHarLry,	Thomas F. Finley and another,	Brackley,
Francis Duncy,	William Young, by Margaret Young, his Mother and Guar.	Tannylack,
Do.,	do.	Drummauple,
Ross McCabe,	Robert J. Burrowes,	Tannylan,
Mary Tate,	do.	Killyreghan,
Benjamin Donaldson,	do.	Corrovoggy,
Catherine O'Brien,	Lord Farnham,	Gola,
Philip Smith,	do.	do.
		Total,

PROVINCE OF

COUNTY OF

CAVAN—continued.

Extent of Holding.	Poor Law Valuation.	Former Rent.	Judicial Rent.	Observations.
A. R. P.	£ s. d.	£ s. d.	£ s. d.	
23 1 30	14 0 0	23 3 2	16 5 0	
15 1 2	9 10 0	9 3 4	4 0 0	
20 3 2	15 0 0	14 8 0	13 0 4	
23 0 26	16 15 0	16 10 0	11 16 0	
13 0 11	6 15 0	6 10 0	5 10 0	
23 0 0	20 0 0	24 6 0	17 0 0	
41 1 36	17 10 0	19 4 0	13 10 0	
13 9 4	7 0 0	7 0 0	3 15 0	
34 0 23	14 0 0	17 0 0	11 15 0	
13 0 36	7 10 0	6 10 0	5 0 0	By consent.
16 1 21	6 5 0	5 14 0	5 0 0	
21 0 20	6 0 0	13 4 3	7 13 0	
64 5 7	34 5 0	56 9 11½	30 10 0	
3 3 23	—	1 14 0	1 5 0	
5 0 64	6 0 0	3 19 3	3 10 0	
16 1 30	14 0 0	15 0 0	11 5 0	
9 1 17	5 5 0	4 0 0	4 10 0	
7 3 23	4 0 0	5 1 0	3 15 0	
634 3 4	228 15 0	253 6 11½	203 9 6	

LEINSTER.

County Court Judge.	No.	Name of Tenant.	Name of Landlord.	Townland.
Gerald Fitzgerald.	294	John Geoghry,	Reps. of Alexander Learmonth,	Kilnarty (part of),

| William Hickman, Q.C. | 347 | John Fagan, | Robert A. Gradvell, | Curhamtown |

J. M. Brunarm	5325	Bryan Henry, and Co.,	Trustees of Rev. W. G. Balling-ham.	Gurthrook,
	5320	Bridget McManmon and another.	do.	do.
				Total,

CONNAUGHT.

MAYO.

	£ s d		£ s d
unartised,	4 15 0		
18 0 10	2 10 0		
18 0 10	4 5 0		

MUNSTER.

CORK.

CIVIL BILL COURTS.

County Court Judge.	No.	Name of Process.	Name of Landlord.	Townland.
B. Ferguson, Q.C.	421	Patrick Mahony,	Donald O'Connell,	Greenhill,
	422	John Reilly,	do.	do.
	423	Andrew MacCarthy,	Catherine A. Donovan,	Knockanegh,
	424	William B. Young,	do.	do.
	425	Patrick Neill, junior,	do.	do.
	426	William Young,	do.	do.
	427	Eliza Hayes,	do.	do.
	428	William B. Young,	do.	do.
	429	Mary Hayes,	Earl of Bandon,	Kilbrogan,
	600	Timothy Mahony,	do.	Knockacushrig,
	601	Jeremiah Mahony and another,	do.	do.
	602	Thomas Bartshum and another,	do.	Mountgould,
	603	James Crawley,	do.	Drumieugh,
	604	Mary Hayes and another,	do.	Killmunson,
				Total,

J. A. Curran, Q.C.				
	423	Michael Cronin,	Lord Listowel,	Ballinagurah,
	424	Thomas Clifford,	Arthur Blennerhassett,	Limerdale,
	425	Pat Carmody,	Earl of Listowel,	Bunia, &c.
	426	Timothy Donoghue,	Thomas R. Moriarty and another,	Finem and another,
	427	Mary Divane,	Francis R. Chute,	Leamhara,
	428	Timothy Sullivan,	Oliver S. Eager,	Glaveegeare,
	429	William O'Connor,	Bess T. Stanghton,	Ardmulan,
	430	John Hannain,	Falkiner G. Sandes,	Leath, East,
	431	Johanna McCarthy,	Captain Oliver Stokes and others,	Ballyhahlm,
	432	Jeremiah Reddy,	do.	do.
	433	Jane Howard,	do.	do.
	434	James Harrington, Rep. of Johanna Harrington,	Thomas K. Sullivan,	Rem,
	435	John Sullivan,	Michael Prendergast,	Caherdran,
	436	Jeremiah Bradley,	Redmond Roche,	Terrenageragh,
	437	Maurice M. Daly,	Earl of Kenmare,	Knockraanabhigh,

Printed using donations by the University of Southampton Library Digitisation Unit

CORK—*continued.*

Areas of Holdings Barato	Poor Law Valuation	Former Rent	Judicial Rent	Observations	Value of Tenancy
A. R. P.	£ s. d.	£ s. d.	£ s. d.		£ s. d.
67 0 0	21 10 0	23 0 0	16 5 0		
63 8 27	23 15 0	26 0 0	19 0 0		
31 1 90	9 10 0	6 0 0	6 0 0		
18 0 50	6 15 0	6 1 1	6 10 0		
41 0 11	11 0 0	16 0 0	11 15 0		
11 3 5	13 0 0	12 3 2	6 10 0		
43 1 31	15 5 0	16 10 0	11 0 0		
20 3 39	6 15 0	6 1 1	6 10 0		
21 0 0	8 13 0	13 16 8	9 0 0		
24 0 0	18 0 0	16 15 0	13 0 0		
63 0 0	28 10 0	23 10 0	18 0 0		
36 1 13	14 10 0	18 18 5	13 0 0		
60 5 30	28 15 0	30 0 0	21 0 0		
35 0 0	18 10 0	15 6 5	11 0 0		
716 3 24	680 13 0	677 17 0	740 10 0		

KERRY.

61 0 25	39 10 0	60 15 2	46 0 0		
9 0 77	5 0 0	5 5 0	6 0 0		
60 6 35	19 15 0	16 0 0	61 0 0	By consent.	
6 3 80	1 10 0	4 0 0	2 0 0		
37 1 3	33 5 0	36 0 0	27 0 0		
3 3 0	0 13 0	6 0 0	1 3 5		
64 3 0	23 15 0	23 10 5	25 15 0		
36 3 31	3 15 0	13 5 0	5 5 0		
15 3 30	6 0 0	6 10 0	7 10 0		
19 3 61	6 5 0	12 15 4	7 10 0		

County Court Judge.	No.	Name of Tenant.	Name of Landlord.	Townland.
J. A. CURRAN, Q.C.	438	Michael Shank, ...	Wilson Gun, ...	... Brosnan, ...
	439	Timothy Leahy, ...	William T. T. Crosbie,	... Knockmoyne and another.
	440	Patrick Murphy, ...	Lord Headley, ...	... Tournageehy, ...
	441	Thomas Murphy, ...	William P. Broderick,	... Kilmainham, East
	442	Mary T. Spillane, ...	Sir John Godfrey, Bart., ...	... Knockavote, ...
	443	John Sullivan and anor.,	Marquis of Lansdowne,	... Derreennablaha,
	444	Mary Sullivan, ...	do. ...	... Drommagortnagh,
	445	Jeremiah Shea, ...	do. ...	... Arden, ...
	446	James Dower, ...	Maurice S. Reidy,	... Cashenn, ...
	447	Daniel Sullivan, ...	do. ...	... Mealigulem, ...
	448	John Sullivan, ...	do. ...	... Derrygihan, ...
	449	Jerry McCarthy & anor.,	do. ...	... Mealigulem, ...
	450	Michael Donoghue, ...	do. ...	... Derrygihan, ...
	451	Michael McCarthy, ...	do. ...	... Mealigulem, ...
				Total ...

Rents fixed upon the Reports of Valuers appointed by the Irish

PROVINCE OF

No.	Name of Tenant.	Name of Landlord.	Townland.
1	John Forde, ...	Duke of Manchester, ...	Mullanvlae, ...

PROVINCE OF

KERRY—*continued.*

Tenant of Holding. Acres.	Poor Law Valuation.	Former Rent.	Judicial Rent.	Observations.	Value of Tenancy.
A. R. P.	£ s. d.	£ s. d.	£ s. d.		£ s. d.
1 2 18	0 3 0	1 10 0	1 10 0		
23 7 0	3 0 0	6 7 2	5 10 0		
51 1 27	14 10 0	20 10 2	17 17 0		
34 7 11	9 10 0	16 0 0	8 8 0		
43 2 6	15 10 0	21 15 0	16 0 0		
60 0 0	4 0 0	8 1 0	4 3 0		
67 3 9	6 0 0	9 6 0	6 7 0		
27 0 34	5 5 0	11 7 0	7 10 0	And half of 15l. 3s. 4r.	
31 0 20	15 10 0	26 0 0	16 0 0		
10 1 37	6 0 0	5 0 0	2 10 0		
13 3 26	4 15 0	4 0 0	3 5 0		
24 0 4	1 15 0	2 0 0	1 15 0		
15 0 13	4 0 0	6 0 0	3 5 0		
24 0 4	1 15 0	3 0 0	1 15 0		
1,108 0 20	316 15 0	464 0 6	637 17 0		

Land Commission on the Joint Applications of Landlords and Tenants.

ULSTER.

ARMAGH.

Extent of Holding. Acres.	Poor Law Valuation.	Former Rent.	Judicial Rent.	Observations.
A. R. P.	£ s. d.	£ s. d.	£ s. d.	
8 3 5	13 10 0	10 1 0	7 10 0	

CONNAUGHT.

GALWAY.

PROVINCE OF MUNSTER

COUNTY OF CORK

IRELAND. LAND COMMISSION—VALUATION.

LAND LAW (IRELAND) ACT, 1887.

LEASEHOLDERS

PROVINCE OF

Name of Assistant Commissioners by whom Cases were decided.	No.	Name of Tenant.	Name of Landlord.	Townland.
Assistant Commissioners— R. Green (Legal). J. H. Webb. A. W. Biggs.	1291	Robert Agnew, ...	William Agnew, ...	Turnashey, —

	No.	Name of Tenant.	Name of Landlord.	Townland.
Head Commission.	447	Thomas Wright and anor.	James G. Bond, ...	Monbury,
	448	Robert Douglas, ...	Miss Catherine Foster, —	Marlacowarra, —
E. Green (Legal). T. Smyth. J. D. McConnell.	449	Bernard Conlan, ...	Peter Doran, ...	Paderrough, —
	450	John Preston, ...	Lord Gosford, ...	Carrickmacduffy.
	451	John O'Toole, ...	William F. Lisalialair, ...	Dalmrrin, —
				Total, —

	No.	Name of Tenant.	Name of Landlord.	Townland.
Head Commission.	333	John Longmore, ...	Sir Robert Hudson, Bart., —	Carlock and anor.
W. F. Bailey (Legal). G. N. Caldwell. G. M. Harvey.	334	Richard Garrell, ...	Marquis of Headfort, ...	Balmbert, —
	335	Owen Woods and anor.	do. ...	Ryabold and anor.
	336	John Porter, ...	do. —	do. —

ULSTER

ANTRIM.

Extent of Holding Acres	Poor Law Valuation.	Former Rent.	Judicial Rent.	
A. R. P.	£ s. d.	£ s. d.	£ s. d.	
9 0 0	unascertained.	8 13 1	6 10 0	By consent

ARMAGH.

16 0 0	12 0 0	7 15 7	12 0 0	The rent is composed of meeting of
1 1 33	unascertained,	9 3 8	1 10 0	
1 1 6	2 10 0	4 7 6	3 10 0	
6 1 20	5 10 0	6 19 5	4 10 0	
5 3 27	unascertained,	4 1 0½	3 10 0	By consent.
30 1 34	20 0 0	29 7 5½	24 0 0	

CAVAN.

COUNTY OF

Names of Assistant Commissioners by whom Cases were decided.	No.	Lands or Estate.	Name of Landlord.	Townland.
Assistant Commissioners—				
W. F. BAILEY (Legal).	357	Peter Farrelly, ...	Marquis of Headfort, ...	Knockbrogie, ...
O. N. CALDWELL.	338	John Tully, surviving in ...	do.	do.
O. M. BARVEY.		name of Catherine Tully.		
	339	Margaret Lynch, Admix. ...	Oliver S. Nugent, ...	Rockaghey, ...
		of Terence Lynch.		
	340	James Conway, ...	Somerset R. Maxwell & anor. ...	Ardkeen, ...
			Trustees of Anthony O'Reilly.	
	341	Philip Coyle, ...	Henry S. Scobey, ...	Dromalleghe, ...
	342	Joseph Byrne, ...	do.	do.
	343	Bernard Kemperty, ...	Lord Farnham, ...	Timmrinan, ...
	344	John Byrne, ...	do.	do.
	345	Thomas Byrne, ...	do.	Aghalaughan, ...
	346	John Byrne, ...	do.	Callaghstown, ...
	347	Christina Sheridan, Admix. ...	Hector E. Burns, ...	Doughorne, Esq.
		wid. of Philip Sheridan.		
	348	R. D. Lynch, ...	Edward Stephenson, ...	Annaharmish, ...
	349	William Byrne, M.D., ...	John E. Curran, ...	Carrickgowna, ...
	350	Thomas McGovern and ...	Thomas Nixby and others, ...	Mornal, ...
		another.		
	351	Michael McGovern, ...	do.	Amberry, ...
	352	James Roberts, ...	Benjamin S. Adams, ...	Lisnabarrigh, ...
	353	Hugh Coey, ...	Marquis of Headfort. ...	Eyebill, ...
				Total, ...

COUNTY OF

CAVAN—*continued*.

Extent of Holding. Statute.	Poor Law Valuation.	Former Rent.	Judicial Rent.	Observations.	Value of Tenancy.
a. r. p.	£ s. d.	£ s. d.	£ s. d.		£ s. d.
26 0 9	17 10 0	20 3 6	16 0 0		
77 0 10	16 10 0	19 0 6	13 10 0		
117 1 5	117 0 0	170 0 0	130 0 0		
91 1 14	6 10 0	10 0 0	7 0 0		
18 0 37	10 10 0	11 0 0	8 0 0		
97 2 17	15 0 0	16 0 0	13 0 0		
80 1 16	11 0 0	17 1 9	11 0 0		
16 2 36	11 5 0	13 5 6	9 0 0		
39 1 18	22 0 0	20 8 3	24 0 0		
26 2 1	14 0 0	16 10 6	13 0 0		
32 1 18	40 0 0	51 8 11	37 0 0		
117 3 31	66 0 0	73 10 0	63 0 0		
77 1 6	22 0 0	20 0 0	19 0 0		
43 3 33	18 10 0	19 1 3	16 10 0		
17 0 0	7 18 0	9 4 3	7 5 0		
18 1 9	16 0 0	11 18 4	9 10 0		
68 1 39	43 5 0	59 1 0	40 0 0	By consent.	
963 2 18	545 3 0	781 13 11	613 0 6		

DOWN.

47 1 3	33 4 0	36 19 1	38 0 6	This tenth holding was fixed by consent of the parties at the sitting of the Court in Dublin.	
5 3 36	6 6 0	4 0 0	3 19 0	do.	
24 3 35	14 4 8	17 10 3	17 15 5	do.	
41 2 16	17 0 0	16 10 0	12 2 6	do.	
5 3 35	7 0 0	6 6 0	6 0 0	do.	
73 2 5	100 0 0	116 4 10	77 8 3		

Digitised by the University of Northampton Library, Digitisation Unit

Names of Assistant Commissioners by whom cases were decided.	No.	Name of Tenant.	Name of Landlord.
Assistant Commissioners—			
S. Green (Legal). T. Davison. J. Patterson.	206	James Sweeny, ...	Richard R. Fleetwood
W. F. Bailey. S. Byrne. J. Patterson.	207	James Lavelle, —	Henry Crawford, & and James Armstrong, his C
W. F. Bailey. T. Davison. J. Patterson.	208	James McEnestey & ors.	William Tumbun,
	209	Patrick Finley, —,	do. —
	210	Catherine Finlay, ...	do. —
	211	Allen Duffy, —	do. —
	212	Michael McCabe, ...	do. —
	213	Owen Finlay, —	do. —
	211	Patrick Duffy, —	do. —

Extra Commission.	657	Joseph McClean, junior,	Colonel J. C. Lowry,
	658	Henry Denby, ...	James Green,
	659	Do., ...	do.
Assistant Commissioners—			
K. Green (Legal). W. G. Byrne. J. Cunningham.	670	Elizabeth Martin, Admix. of Thornton Martin	Amy H. Beeley, & twin W. L. B. Leahy and her Grantham,
	671	Patrick Coffman, ...	do. ...
	672	William Auchinleck, ...	do. —
	673	John Ash, ...	do. ...
	674	Samuel Craignalls, ...	do. ...
	675	Newberry Wilson, ...	do. —
	676	Matthew Wilson, ...	do. ...
	677	Robert Craigmillar, ...	do. —
	678	James Mason, ...	Earl of Belmore, or
	679	James Orr, ...	R. P. Hamilton & as trees of Wm. Smith George R. Blank,
	680	Patrick McCaHey, senior,	...
	681	Peter Devlin, ...	The William &c.

13 0 0	28 5 10	10 15 0	The rent in consequence of sitting of
9 5 0	5 13 10	5 0 0	
8 8 0	9 3 0	7 10 0	
unascertained,	51 12 8	51 0 0	
18 0 0	17 10 6	16 0 0	
10 15 0	7 18 0	7 0 0	By consent.
14 13 0	15 8 0	13 4 0	do.
8 13 0	9 12 5	7 15 0	
23 0 0	24 13 4	19 10 0	do.
17 10 0	17 13 0	15 5 0	do.
7 5 0	9 10 0	5 10 0	
25 20 0	24 4 5	15 10 0	
43 10 0	34 13 0	33 10 0	
7 5 0	9 10 6	9 10 0	do.
13 0 0	8 15 5	7 19 0	
10 10 0	9 16 5	5 10 0	

PROVINCE OF

Name of Assistant Commissioners by whom Court were certified.	No.	Name of Tenant.	Name of Landlord.	Townland.
Assistant Commissioners— R. R. Kane (Legal). W. de La Poer. J. Havernworth.	443	John Anghmy, ...	Philip J. Sevine, ...	Kilcavrig —

Name of Assistant Commissioners—	No.	Name of Tenant.	Name of Landlord.	Townland.
R. R. Kane (Legal). R. Mowbray. B. Carrin.	319	David Bellamy, ...	Colonel M. W. S. Caulfield,	Backstown and another.
	320	Alexander R. Grayden,	Trustees of Morgan's Charity School.	Newcastle, —
R. R. Kane (Legal). R. Mowbray. R. Martin.	321	Patrick Lambey, ...	Sir Nathaniel A. Staples, Bt.,	Killuck, ...
	322	Robert E. Gibson, ...	Miss Anne Clarke, ...	Westmanstown & another.
	323	Patrick McDonnell, ...	Lord Cloncurry, ...	Castlewarden, —
	324	Patrick Harvey, continued in name of John Harvey.	do. — ...	Colmanstown, ...
	325	Catherine Kelly, ...	Joseph Gorman, — ...	Newcastle, —
	326	Edward Quin, —	Colonel James F. Fowler, —	Orange, ...
	327	Mary Doyle, continued in name of Francis Doyle.	Lord Cloncurry, ...	Ashgrove Hill Farm,
	328	John Dunne, —	Baron de Robeck, ...	Newtown, ...
				Total, —

LEINSTER.

CARLOW.

Acres of Holding Sold.	Poor Law Valuation.	Former Rent.	Judicial Rent.	Observations.	Value of Tenancy.
A. R. P.	£ s. d.	£ s. d.	£ s. d.		£ s. d.
88 3 14	43 0 0	137 0 0	78 0 0		

DUBLIN.

182 3 0	348 15 0	230 3 4	220 3 4		
161 3 6	849 5 0	890 0 0	890 0 0		
71 0 32	13 0 0	53 0 0	15 0 0		
134 1 15	758 0 9	245 13 6	180 0 0		
128 3 25	184 0 8	195 0 0	148 0 0		
53 0 24	73 10 0	91 0 1	75 0 0		
4 3 17	4 0 0	7 17 6	8 0 0		
16 0 30	91 0 0	73 0 0	14 0 0		
62 1 25	45 0 0	68 17 10	69 0 0	By consent.	
114 2 11	178 0 0	141 0 0	131 0 0	do.	
872 2 8½	1,068 5 0	1,453 18 3	1,133 5 4		

Names of deferred Commissioners by whom Cases were decided	No.	Name of Tenant	Name of Landlord	Townland
HEAD COMMISSIONER.	344	Andrew E. McCracken, occnpr. in pstce of David R. Thola, his Assignee.	Government Hewetson's School Chest, County Kildare.	Donaghtown,
	345	Esther Harkaness,	Captain Theresa Blake,	Clonmines Roos,
	346	Mathew Malin,	Rev. Wm. M. Clohar, p.p.	Old Kilcullen,
	347	Do.	do.	do.
Assistant Commissioners— D. H. Kean (Legal), R. Marsh, W. S. Hurst.	348	Michael Cholan, Admgr. of Michael Conlan.	Sarah M. Rice and others,	Leckagh,
	349	Justin Dempsey,	Henry A. Keogh,	Knocklishgoiman
	350	Bernard Nowl,	Thomas Baugh,	Proudstown,
	351	Thomas Nolan,	do.	Johnstown,
	352	Catherine Murphy,	do.	do.
	353	Johanna Murphy,	do.	do.
	354	Richard McDonald,	do.	Proudstown,
	355	Joseph Brennan,	do.	Johnstown,
	356	Patrick Byrne,	do.	do.
	357	James Byrne,	do.	do.
	358	Margaret Lawler,	Joseph E. D. Drake,	Tumin,
	359	Elizabeth Minch, Admx. of Patrick Minch.	Miss Annette Hyden,	Ballyvoghta,
	360	Luke Miller,	Thomas Hewetson, ensed. in rstate of Algernon Aylmer,	Curraneetown,
	361	Thomas Nolan,	Frederick L. Fitzgerald,	Plunkettstown, in
	362	Do.	do.	do.
	363	Eliza Flaherty,	do.	Knockpatrick,
	364	Thomas Doyle,	do.	Plunkettstown,
	365	William S. Coates,	do.	Knocknanaugh
	366	Michael Cope,	do.	Ballyveggan,
	367	John Moody,	John LaTouche,	Rathmooney,
	368	Thomas Keatley,	do.	Rathangain,
	369	John McNally,	do.	Clonsuin,
	370	James Leigh,	do.	Blackrath,
	371	Denis Murphy,	Thomas Butler,	Ballymoor,
	372	Andrew Murphy,	Timothy Byrne,	Ballululain,
	373	Michael Racy,	Mrs. Mary J. Miller,	Moone,
	374	William Knight,	Marquis of Drogheda,	Clonoggeth,

Printed image digitised by the University of Southampton Library Digitisation Unit

KILDARE.

Ext. of Holding. Acres.	Poor Law Valuation.	Former Rent.	Judicial Rent.	Observations.	Value of Tenancy.
A. R. P.	£ s. d.	£ s. d.	£ s. d.		£ s. d.
137 8 19	89 5 0	100 0 0	90 0 0	The rent in this case was fixed by consent of the parties at the sitting of the Court in Dublin.	
19 9 15	16 6 0	19 17 3	16 10 0	do.	
20 0 21	7 10 0	13 0 0	9 0 0	do.	
10 0 6	4 5 0	18 10 0	9 10 0	do.	
55 9 14	57 10 0	84 9 6	61 0 0		
166 2 84	93 0 0	210 0 0	135 0 0		
56 2 50	58 15 0	43 0 0	58 0 0		
121 2 52	47 10 0	50 0 0	42 0 0		
37 3 29	23 5 0	87 7 0	83 0 0		
37 0 0	37 15 0	29 17 0	33 9 0		
27 1 57	50 10 0	24 10 0	34 10 0		
185 0 57	83 15 0	78 11 9	63 0 9		
70 9 15	39 13 0	28 15 4	50 0 0		
44 1 57	83 15 0	79 13 9	27 0 0		
151 1 0	83 0 0	180 0 0	115 9 0		
17 2 34	7 13 0	10 9 0	5 10 0		
175 1 0	121 11 0	147 5 5	180 6 0		
7 1 5	uncertain,	7 5 6	4 0 6		
16 2 25	do.	15 10 0	9 0 0		
86 1 57	82 15 9	37 0 0	24 0 0		
84 0 0	50 5 0	48 0 0	27 0 0		
194 7 25	80 0 0	160 0 0	100 0 0		
61 9 7	uncertain,	15 0 0	18 0 0		
101 0 0	43 0 0	49 7 4	45 0 0		
50 7 18	24 10 0	11 5 0	23 0 0		
85 0 0	17 5 0	17 5 0	14 0 0		
99 8 7	60 0 0	78 0 0	88 0 0		
85 6 11	14 10 0	13 0 0	13 0 0		
5 5 17	3 10 0	6 0 0	4 0 0		
113 2 25	46 0 0	50 0 0	47 0 0		
54 0 11	69 0 0	76 0 0	63 0 0		

Names of Assistant Commissioners by whom Cases were decided	No.	Name of Tenant	Name of Landlord	Townland.
Assistant Commissioners:—				
R. R. Kane (Legal). R. Martin. W. S. Hurt.	673	Timothy Byrne,	John Graves, senid. in trust of Thomas Graves	Ballahalea,
	674	Margaret Lawler,	Frederick M. Carroll,	Kerns,
R. R. Kane (Legal). S. Mourmay. P. Callan.	377	John Quinn,	Mrs. Jane Newcomen,	Leixlip,
	376	Do.,	Clara E. Spalman,	Ballymakealy,
	676	Patrick J. Dunne,	Lord Rathdonnell,	Aghard,
	380	John Danford,	Very Rev. Arthur J. Hunter and others,	Rawtown,
	381	George Alexander,	Colonel M. Can'field,	Clonkwenten Park,
	382	William Watson,	Right Hon. Henry Bruen and another, Trustees of late Thomas Connolly,	Oldtown,
	383	John Danford,	Very Rev. Thomas Hare,	Collinstown and another.
R. R. Kane (Legal). A. R. Drake. P. Callan.	384	Hugh McCormick,	Miss F. A. de Ryder,	Clondown,
	385	Robert Hannegan,	John F. Gunn,	Punchur's Grange,
	386	Mrs. Ellen Loughlin,	do.	do.
	827	Stephen Byrne,	Joseph M. Neale,	Christianstown,
	328	William Farrell,	Denis J. H. Cronin,	Stephenstown,
R. R. Kane (Legal). R. Martin. A. R. Drake.	329	Hugh Cullen,	Samuel W. Haughton,	Mullaghmast,
R. R. Kane (Legal). P. Callan.	390	William A. Wells,	Lord Cloncurry,	Northumberland
	391	William A. Wells and others,	do.	Newpark,
	892	Thomas Newnham,	Captain Francis W. Brown,	Balport,
	893	Laurence Nugent, senid. in trust of Walter Nugent,	do.	Balnahesk,
	894	Martin Dunne,	do.	Portnahon,
	396	Henry Byrne,	Fleetwood Byrd,	Moortown & anor
				Total

KILDARE—*continued*

Extent of Holding. Statute.	Poor Law Valuation.	Former Rent.	Judicial Rent.	Observations.
A. R. P.	£ s. d.	£ s. d.	£ s. d.	
153 3 34	77 15 0	82 13 10	75 0 0	
47 1 22	33 10 0	66 8 0	28 0 0	
15 3 29	17 15 0	18 0 0	20 10 0	
15 0 0	10 16 0	12 0 5	15 0 5	
46 2 11	47 0 0	57 0 0	54 0 0	
54 1 6	44 0 0	50 0 0	60 0 0	
296 6 77	471 0 0	442 3 3	410 0 0	
43 3 4	55 16 0	90 0 0	42 0 0	
57 3 33	38 0 0	43 0 0	28 0 0	
71 0 61	83 10 0	90 0 0	85 0 0	
211 0 12	143 7 0	198 5 1	160 0 0	By consent.
134 3 16	120 10 0	133 0 0	120 10 0	do.
71 1 3	48 0 0	53 0 0	45 0 0	do.
157 1 38	60 0 0	57 0 0	60 0 0	do.
183 1 50	111 15 0	173 0 0	140 0 0	
840 5 30	318 5 0	256 10 0	210 0 0	
94 3 7	94 0 0	116 0 0	88 0 0	
67 3 33	70 0 0	73 3 3	73 0 0	
36 3 13	61 10 0	43 14 4	79 0 0	
60 0 30	47 10 0	51 6 0	43 0 0	
36 0 33	73 10 0	100 0 0	33 0 0	
3,133 1 16	3,125 4 0	3,833 5 3	3,105 0 5	

COUNTY OF

Names of Assistant Commissioners by whom Cases were decided.	No.	Name of Tenant.	Name of Landlord.	Townland.
Assistant Commissioners:—				
J. H. Eson (Legal). A. N. Coyne. J. H. Butar.	460	Michael Sexton, —	Francis F. Tydd, —	Grovine, East, —
	461	James Hennessy, —	do. —	do. —
	462	Mrs. Anne Brennan, —	William Darcy, —	Kilshany —
	463	William Manning, —	John Byrne, —	Agher, —
	464	Robert Madigan, —	Mrs. Anne J. Andrews, —	Pickmoss, —
	465	Martin Bridget, —	Mrs. Margaret Sullivan, —	Bourmin, —
	466	Martin Carroll, —	do. —	do. —
	467	Christopher Agar, —	William J. G. Doyle, —	Ballyvalla, —
	468	Lindesay Knox, —	Lackin G. Bendy, —	Monrigole, —
	469	James Bergin, —	Edward Holohan, another in name of Edward Holohan —	Leggetterath and another, —
	470	Mary Meany, Ltd. Admix. of William Meany,	do. —	Callanstown, La, —
	471	Thomas J. Lalor and others, Trustees of Pierce Murphy,	do. —	Leggetterath, —
	472	Do. —	do. —	Aughmaing, —
	473	Johanna Shortall, Ltd. Admix. of John Shortall and another,	do. —	Leggetterath, —
	474	Patrick Kenlly, —	do. —	do. —
			Total, —	

KING'S

Assistant Commissioners:—	No.			
M. T. Cerar (Legal), K. Devereux, G. H. Montge,	515	Edward Lynham, —	J. C. G. Armit, —	Millcown, —
	316	William Killen, —	Lord Ashbrooke, —	Eagles, —
	320	Peter Wyns, —	Joshua Smithers, —	Ballyryan, —
	521	Andrew Brack, —	Agnes Daly and another, —	Croghan, —
	522	William Murphy, junior,	John Wakely, —	Dunville, —
	523	Mrs. Mary A. Clarke, —	Benjamin M. Ball, —	Bakinshill, —
	524	George Gilliard, —	Robert Lucas, —	Ballybin and another, —
	525	Kate Saunderson and others,	Henry G. Joly and others, —	Kilkeow, —
	526	Do. —	do. —	do. —
			Total, —	

Former Rent	Judicial Rent	Observations	Value of Tenancy
£ s. d.	£ s. d.		£ s. d.
77 7 6	94 0 8		
59 18 3	43 0 6		
100 0 0	69 0 0		
6 10 0	5 5 6		
60 19 1	35 10 0		
43 5 0	34 0 0		
18 2 1	16 0 0		
74 18 0	29 0 0		
180 1 5	180 1 3		
49 1 0	59 0 0		
37 0 0	27 8 0		
31 3 0	34 0 0		
21 10 0	15 0 0		
36 0 0	23 0 0		
10 0 0	7 10 0		

Names of Assistant Commissioners by whom Cases were decided.	No.	Name of Tenant.	Name of Landlord.	Townland.
Head Commissioner.	512	Peter Roche,	Charles G. Stannell and others, Trustees of James Tunnell.	Ballygunner
	513	Walter Morrissey,	Sir G. M. Foster, Bart., reminder by Tom H. Foster and others, Trustees of Sir A. W. Foster, Bart., in addition.	Monianebolen
Assistant Commissioners— W. F. Bailey (Legal). C. W. Thompson. J. R. Heazer.	514	Ross Hassett, Urquhart Admr. of Michael Biscuit,	Plunkett Henry, Guardian of Mary Kenny, a lunatic.	Corkan
	515	Patrick Shaughlan,	do.	do.
				Total,

Names of Assistant Commissioners by whom Cases were decided.	No.	Name of Tenant.	Name of Landlord.	Townland.
Head Commissioner.	633	Edward McKeever,	Marquis Conyngham,	Mullaghilin, —
	634	James Cogan,	Colonel J. N. Coddington,	Mullaghvea, —
	635	Samuel Wilson,	Robert G. Dunville,	Loughanmore, —
	636	James May,	do.	Rathleigh, —
	637	Mary Bradley,	Earl of Fingall, —	Williamstown, —
	638	John Lynch,	Mrs. Margaret Creagh,	The Biggins —
	639	Nicholas Reilly,	Major A. J. Preston,	Dunestown and another.
Assistant Commissioners— W. E. Bailey (Legal). J. O'Callaghan. L. J. Kennedy.	640	Patrick Casty and anor.	Rev. Thomas Allen, —	Mansfield, —
	641	Edward Gilshenan, —	do. —	Dogstown and another.
	642	Michael Gilshenan, —	do. —	Mansfield, —
	643	Patrick Cosgrave and others.	Robert Fowler, —	Glanstown —
E. R. Shaw (Legal). K. Sullivan. R. Martin.	644	Christopher McCornick,	Colonel James F. Forster, —	Ellistown and another.
	645	Joseph Chapman, —	Edward R. Woods, —	Moynalty and son.
	646	Thomas O'Connor, —	Ferdinand McVeagh, —	Coolgush, —
R. R. Kane (Legal). R. Murray.	647	John McCarthy, —	Peter Moran, —	Dunshaughlin, —
	648	Patrick Scully, —	Nathaniel F. Preston, —	K.Dale, —
				Total, —

Printed under direction of the University of Southampton Library Digitisation Unit

TABLE OF JUDICIAL RENTS.

Former Rent.	Judicial Rent.	
£ s. d.	£ s. d.	
175 0 0	125 0 0	The rent in general sitting of
250 16 3	200 0 0	
9 5 0	6 6 0	
3 0 0	3 0 0	
416 11 3	343 6 0	

200 0 0	160 0 0	The rent in general sitting o
114 6 8	92 10 0	
64 13 10	59 0 0	
73 6 7	70 0 0	
43 3 4	37 0 0	
50 0 0	29 0 0	
123 13 8	105 0 0	
60 6 0	61 0 0	By command
88 6 0	70 0 0	do.
90 16 6	62 0 0	do.
81 13 5	66 0 0	do.

QUEEN'S

Name of Assistant Commissioner by whom Cases were decided	No.	Name of Tenant	Name of Landlord	Townland
Assistant Commissioners:—				
H. B. Rawe (Legal), W. S. Hane, R. Morris.	312	Kate Quinlan,	Lord Congleton,	Slate, Lewis,
	313	James Loughon,	Rev. George W. Gregory,	Ballaghbeg,
	320	Edward McGee,	do.	do.
	321	Patrick Kinava,	do.	Ballaghmore,
W. S. Hane, R. Martin.	322	Winifred Whelan,	Colonel Robert G. Cosby,	Oakpain,
	323	Do.	do.	Clonreynaghagh,
J. H. Edge (Legal), R. Chaney, R. B. Ferguson.	324	Daniel Byrne,	Colonel William T. Dobson,	Lisdugney,
	325	Thomas Byrne,	Major E. G. Cosby,	Aughaderry,
	326	Thomas Howard,	William Filkington,	Kilmurry,
				Total,

COUNTY OF

Assistant Commissioners:—	No.	Name of Tenant	Name of Landlord	Townland
E. B. Kirk (Legal), H. F. Simson, C. E. Petrie.	304	Thomas Weir,	Baths Leslie Nugent,	Walshestown,
	353	John Gilmore,	Mrs. Emily J. Tyrrell,	Robinstown, Tyrrellsrath,
	360	Lewis Phelan, copied to the name of Brady by F. Johnston,	Earl of Longford,	Carrickboro and another,
	362	Matilda C. Doran,	do.	Wardfort,
	368	Mary Doran,	do.	Queryfarragh and another,
	369	Gerald J. Byrne,	do.	Riverstown,
	370	Thomas Glynn,	do.	Clonlishroek,
	371	Mary Kerry, Admin. of Thomas Kerry, dead.	Major E. Murphy,	Rathcallagh,
	372	Thomas Cleary,	John F. Bamford,	Clondiff,
	373	Robert Fox,	Captain B. Swipe, copied to name of Deborah J. Swipe,	Glenshey,
	374	Esther Murray, copied in name of Michl. Murray,	Margaret H. Ledvon,	Deepdink,
	375	Jasper F. McCionnach,	General Ledviss, &c., copied in name of Mrs. Emily Ledviss,	Balgarrett,
	376	Lawrence Kelly,	John Malone,	Castletown Geoghegan,
	377	Walter Hins, Admin. of the late Richard Hins.	John R. F. G. Tuthill,	Clohenny,
				Total,

	Former Rent.	Judicial Rent.	Observations.	
d.	*£ s. d.*	*£ s. d.*		*£ s. d.*
0	114 18 9	100 0 0		
0	25 0 0	18 0 0		
0	220 0 0	145 0 0		
0	11 18 8	8 16 0		
and,	13 11 0	10 18 0		
0	5 0 0	4 10 0		
0	101 10 0	75 0 0	By consent.	
0	9 0 7	6 6 8	do.	
0	457 0 0	281 6 7	do.	
0	1,007 17 9	683 7 10		

0	80 0 0	80 0 0		
0	30 0 0	20 0 0		
0	330 0 0	285 0 0		
0	120 0 0	116 0 0		
0	90 0 0	80 0 0		
0	90 0 0	75 0 0		
0	22 0 0	18 0 0		
0	24 18 0	21 0 0		
0	123 7 8	118 0 0		
0	25 2 10	23 0 0		
0	44 18 0	99 0 0		
0	554 13 3	470 0 0		
0	40 0 0	33 0 0		
0	170 8 0	145 0 0		
0	1,775 2 9	1,547 0 0		

IRISH LAND COMMISSION.

Names of Assistant Commissioners by whom Cases were decided.	No.	Name of Tenant.	Name of Landlord.	Townland.
Head Commission.	318	John Kelpie,	Matthew A. Maher,	Ballyagheen, Upr.
	319	Joshua Scott,	General E. Richards,	Ballydineen,
Assistant Commissioners—	331	Ellen Murphy,	Gabriel J. W. Rodgomel,	Ballyheen,
J. H. Shaw (Legal). M. P. Lynch. W. Wallace.	330	Francis Guilfoide,	Captain E. T. Irvine,	Kilshannaroghes,
	353	Thomas Nolan,	Margaret Templdin,	Kilstophen,
	354	Joseph Rooney,	Lady Adelaide Fitzgerald,	Clonpowns, Far.
	355	Michael Davy,	do.	Ballydonghlin,
	406	Margaret Colburne,	John H. Whitcroft,	Ballymoran,
	407	John Kinsella,	Randhiam J. Byrne and others,	Ballyhanny,
	408	John Rutherford,	do.	do.
	409	Michael Kinsella,	do.	do.
	410	Ellen Fitzpatrick, Wife of Joseph Fitzpatrick,	Rev. John D. Pennon & son,	Ballyrahinrain,
	431	Michael Leavy,	William W. Gibbon,	Ballybeg Great,
	432	Mathew Doyle,	do.	Jenebeg,
	463	Patrick Cody,	N. R. Cockman,	Monart, East,
	464	Mary Kinnett,	Mrs. Kate Kinnett,	Rocksboyscourt,
	465	Mary Kanjuar (Widow),	Lettice A. Bryan,	Ballyshiadle,
	466	Ellen Whitmore,	John B. Sparrow, acted in name of James McWilliams and another,	Frankfort,
	467	Denis Kehoe,	John K. Battersby,	Clonbrien,
	549	Margaret Pierce,	Earl of Courtown,	Clologe,
	550	Richard Greene,	do.	Knockmulin, Lr.
	570	Do.	do.	do.
	571	Do.	do.	do.
	572	Do.	do.	Knockmulin, Upr.
	573	Thomas Rowinhen,	J. A. Macaneny and others, Assignees of William Bolton, a Bankrupt.	Ballymhmund,
				Total

TABLE OF JUDICIAL RENTS

Former Rent.	Judicial Rent.	Observations
£ s. d.	£ s. d.	
9 15 2	7 0 0	The rent in this case exclusive of the pro- ceeding of the Court &c.
18 0 0	8 5 0	
33 16 8	28 0 0	
46 0 0	41 0 8	
70 17 8	60 0 0	By agreement.
10 8 4	8 0 0	do.
16 10 8	13 10 0	do.
46 0 0	54 0 0	do.
20 0 0	11 0 0	
19 0 0	13 8 0	
18 6 8	10 0 0	
101 8 8	86 15 0	
13 2 6	10 6 7	

IRISH LAND COMMISSION.

Names of Assistant Commissioners by whom Cases were decided.	No.	Name of Tenant.	Name of Landlord.	Townland.
Head Commissioner.	431	Mathew Moore,	... Earl of Carysfort,	— Killnacher,
	432	Bryant W. B. Fortloy,	Earl Fitzwilliam, —	.. Newcastle Lower, and another.
	433	William Newland,	do. ...	— Herbertstown, Lower.
	434	Ralph Lawrence,	do. —	— Upper Ballyagan and another.
	435	Edward Craddock,	do. —	.. Dunhert. —
Assistant Commissioners—	436	Thomas Real,	— Robert G. Wade,	... Ballingrein and another.
R. R. Hare (Legal). W. G. De la Poer. J. Hawksworth.	437	Harcourt Lees,	... Thomas Bowen,	.— Kilquade, —
	438	John O'Neill,	.. Henry Goodham,	... Ballyhamee, —
	439	Thomas W. Darby,	... do. —	— Ballyhanue Annesley.
	440	Michael Keenan,	... Rev. Thomas A. G. Draught,	Ashtown & another.
	441	Elizabeth M. Clarke, Limited Admix. of John T. Clarke.	Armitage R. Humphreys, —	M'Garvey, —
	442	Thomas Winder,	... Colonel M. J. Haygarr, xxxtd. in name of Mrs. Mary S. Haytan and another.	Tonreen, —
	443	John Manly,	... Thomas Aston, —	... Cardenstown, —
				Total, —

Assistant Commissioners—	799	James Nolan,	... Thomas R. Lahiff and another,	Glenhaugh —
J. G. Gerrs, q.c. (Legal). W. A. Burr. H. G. Nash.	800	John Feeney,	... Josephine Burke and another, Reps. of late Dominick Burke.	Tobberbracken—
	801	Andrew Bagier,	— Major-General W. S. Cooper,	Lackyle, —
	802	Michael Moore,	— W. S. T. Holmes,	— Islandmore, —

* Printed image, digitised by the University of Southampton Library Digitisation Unit

WICKLOW.

Extent of Holding Groups.	Poor Law Valuation.			Tenure Rent.			Judicial Rent.		
A. R. P.	£	s.	d.	£	s.	d.	£	s.	d.
91 1 28	23	10	0	13	18	4	28	0	0
207 3 61	231	15	0	286	0	0	253	0	0
247 2 21	160	15	0	207	0	0	170	0	0
453 3 53	315	5	0	315	0	0	273	0	0
164 1 85	110	0	0	122	10	0	100	0	0
167 2 21	181	0	0	214	10	0	120	0	0
35 1 5	50	0	0	68	5	0	47	0	0
90 3 33	54	0	0	100	0	0	55	0	0
106 1 94	110	0	0	144	0	0	100	0	0
141 2 0	54	10	0	50	0	0	28	0	0
533 2 13	194	0	0	330	0	0	140	0	0
653 1 53	354	0	0	347	19	2	182	0	0
97 3 63	38	0	0	20	18	0	88	18	0
3,156 0 1	1,745	13	0	2,055	14	8	1,653	13	0

CONNAUGHT.

GALWAY.

IRISH LAND COMMISSION.

Name of Assistant Commissioner in whose Court cases detailed.	No.	Name of Tenant.	Name of Landlord.	Townland.
Assistant Commissioner—				
M. T. OMAR (Legal).	303	Miss Kenney,	Right Hon. Francis McClintock and others,	Rannaville,
R. McOWEN.	304	John Conneely,	Francis O'T. B. Foster,	Clonkeevy,
A. R. RAVENSCROFT.	305	Michael O'Sullivan, junr.	Frederic L. Chapin,	Aughnamony,
	306	Mary Cummings, Reps. of Patrick Cummins,	Major John de B. Lynch,	Carrowkelly,
	307	Very Rev. C. H. G. Rahan,	Colonel J. A. Daly,	Kaiskanganna,
	308	Patrick Shaughnessy and another,	Martin Redkin,	Larkagh,
	309	Giles F. Lambert,	William H. P. Trenchell,	Kinn,
	310	Edward J. Madden,	Robert J. Martin,	Suke,
	311	Charles O. Ottilingham,	do.	Delmaun,
	312	Peter Webbe,	Colonel H. Clements,	Marmsgowagh,
	313	Do.	do.	Lun,
M. T. OMAR (Legal).	314	James Sked,	John W. McConchy and anor., Assignees of Henry Clinton,	K.Ukroch, Esq.,
J. T. DAVIS.	315	John Smyth,	Mrs. Mary B. Longstaff,	Corryboghals,
M. DAVEY.	316	Ellen Kiely,	Patrick S. Corcellin,	Ballintogra,
	317	Patrick Walsh,	do.	Millpark,
	318	Myles Walsh,	Lord Clonbrock,	Lisochill,
	319	Benjamin Taylor,	do.	Coinnanside,
	320	Martin Clements, Reps. of Marty Clemens,	do.	Lisochill,
	321	John Clemence, Lth. Admor. of Thos. Clemence,	do.	do.
	322	Lawrence M. Egan,	do.	do.
	323	Bridget Robinson,	do.	Littlewood,
	324	James Farrell,	do.	Lisochill,
	325	James Moylan,	do.	do.
	326	Bridget Clemence, Lth. Admor. of Thos. Clemence,	do.	do.
	327	William Hardy,	do.	Ballycooney,
	328	Thomas Dwyer, Rep. of Luke Dwyer,	do.	Lisochill,
	329	Peter B. Burke,	James Haigh,	Moyglass,
	330	Mary Daly,	Peter R. Burke,	do.
	331	John Dudgan,	do.	do.
	332	Bridget Dudgan,	do.	do.
	333	Patrick Madden,	Denis S. Daly,	Carrowren,
	334	Thomas Tully,	George H. Whichcote and anr.	Killneen,
				Total

50	0	0	70	0	0
80	0	0	15	0	0
100	0	0	43	0	0
180	0	0	85	0	0

3	5	0	1	15	0
150	0	0	80	0	0
62	1	0	20	15	0
72	0	6	15	15	0
25	6	3	30	10	0
20	10	11	72	0	0
10	0	3	9	10	0
11	6	9	9	10	0

Name of Assistant Commissioners by whom Cases were Settled.	No.	Name of Tenant.	Name of Landlord.
Assistant Commissioners—			
D. TULLY (Legal).	528	Patrick Fox, ...	Colonel M. F. Comyn,
R. JOHNSTON.	545	Do.	do.
C. O'KEEFE.	570	Anne Rhandron, ...	do.
	571	The Irish (No. 2 Series, (Possessory) Building Society,	George Marsham,
	572	Ferrall Brady, ...	James F. O'Brien,
	575	James Mundy, ...	Miss Henrietta O'Brien, in count of. Mrs. and C.

Assistant Commissioners—	128	Elizabeth McClung, ...	Earl of Lucan, ...
D. TULLY (Legal).			
R. SPROULE.			
S. WILSON.			
D. TULLY (Legal).	152	John Burkett and anor.,	Major D. R. Fair,
R. R. BURTON.			
R. O'KEEFE.	176	Robert Crown, ...	Mrs. Mary Anne Shaw,

TABLE OF JUDICIAL RENTS.

Former Rent	Judicial Rent	
£ s. d.	£ s. d.	
9 15 0	6 5 0	
21 4 9	16 10 0	
31 0 0	5 10 0	
67 0 9	57 0 9	

PROVINCE OF

COUNTY OF

Name of Assistant Commissioners by whom Case was decided.	No.	Name of Tenant.	Name of Landlord.	Townland.
Assistant Commissioners—				
J. R. Greer, Q.C. (Legal).	1085	Patrick Hogan, ...	George O'C. Westropp, —	Coolroughmore,
W. R. Hunt,	1086	Patrick Minogue, —	Captain G. D. Sampson, —	Kielty, —
H. G. Nash.	1087	Patrick Tuohy, ...	William N. Westropp, ...	Dromore, —
	1088	Patrick Minogue, ...	do. ...	Derryfill, —
	1089	John Hickey, —	John Scanlan and others, —	Ballynalacken, —
J. B. Greene, M.P. (Legal).	1090	Denis Guilan, —	John Goodhugo and another,	Quarrin, —
F. Maxwell.	1091	Patrick Liddane, ...	do. —	do. —
J. Simmonds.	1092	Simon Crowe, —	William G. V. Burton, —	Thomastown, —
	1093	Catherine Minogue, Ltd. Admr. of John Minogue	do. ...	Tuilig, —
	1094	Michael Moudes, —	do. ...	Moyadderagh,
	1095	Patrick Spillany, —	do. ...	Thomastown, —
				Tood, —

COUNTY OF

TABLE OF JUDICIAL RENTS.

Former Rent.	Judicial Rent.	Observations.
£ s. d.	£ s. d.	
77 7 1	54 0 0	
1 10 0	1 10 0	
20 0 0	17 0 0	
18 0 0	15 0 0	
6 0 0	6 0 0	

IRISH LAND COMMISSION.

Names of Assistant Commissioners by whom Cases were decided.	No.	Name of Tenant.	Name of Landlord.	Townland.
Assistant Commissioners—				
L. DOYLE (Legal). W. WALPOLE. O. VANSTON.	3542	William Coakley & anor.	Jeremiah O'Donovan,	Lahinalingh
	3544	John Mahony,	Charles L. Furlong,	Killeen
	3548	Patrick Harrington,	Lord Charles P. P. Clinton,	Gossquin
	3544	Andrew McCarthy,	Mrs. G. H. T. Mundy,	Kerrigmore
	4582	Timothy Houston,	Captain J. R. Wheeler,	Kilbeigh
	3585	Michael Barret,	Sir George Colthurst, Bart.,	Killnagarny
	3544	Denis Denton,	Samuel Hadden, surrabend in trust of Aveie H. Cashin,	Carhelly
	3545	Samuel Cotrell,	Captain W. R. W. Sweetman,	Lahanaghmore
	3526	Dowling L. Gotmell,	do.	do.
	3540	John Hemming and anor.	Justin McCarthy,	Kilbraghan
	3543	Bartholomew Callaghan,	do.	do.
	3559	John O'Connor and anor.	do.	do.
	3540	Michael Murphy,	do.	do.
	3543	Johannah Ryan and anor.	do.	do.
	3548	Patrick Riordan,	do.	do.
L. DOYLE (Legal). J. J. GOTY. M. KELLY.	3545	Margaret Collins,	Sir Robert Synge, Bart.,	Liskee Cohee
	3544	William Deasy,	Mrs. Deas Malcom, managed by convent College, McCarthy,	Ballyroufe
	3544	John O'Hea and another,	Miss Nina M. A. Townes,	Liaspadreen
	3544	Maurice Sheehy,	do.	do.
	3547	Mary Desmond,	Munster and Leinster Bank, Limited,	Clonbonnebig
	3549	Do.,	do.	Cloughmnildoin
	3548	Do.,	do.	Maccooran
	3552	Do.,	do.	Kasolinbrough
	3554	Do.,	do.	Cappanrasta, Ind.
	3452	George Barahlet,	do.	do.
	4553	Do.,	do.	Cluhinartdig
	3454	John McCarthy,	do.	Sandhill
	3558	Patrick Crowley,	Benjamin Scott,	Ardnacer
	3558	Florence McCarthy, with admr. of Timothy McCarthy.	Mrs. Eliza Maghery,	Farranagark
	3552	Richard Wood,	Captain A. Perry,	Castlebate
	3558	John Donovan,	Very Rev. Hamus T. Fleming,	Boggura
	3549	Owen Ringwold,	Daniel Connor,	Greenmiddle

TABLE OF JUDICIAL RENTS

CORK—continued

Area of Holding, Statute.	Poor Law Valuation.	Former Rent.	Judicial Rent.	Observations.
a. r. p.	£ s. d.	£ s. d.	£ s. d.	
45 0 35	9 16 0	15 5 0	9 5 8	With right of grazing on the 30s.
49 1 15	18 10 0	19 0 0	18 0 0	With right of grazing on 240s. &c. life.
43 2 16	19 15 0	44 0 0	34 0 0	With right of grazing on the Mountain.
18 3 37	8 0 0	10 0 0	7 15 0	
43 0 25	12 0 0	16 0 0	13 0 0	By consent.
319 2 12	123 0 0	184 7 0	138 12 4	do.
57 0 4	81 1 0	63 0 0	33 0 9	do.
49 3 12	81 0 0	58 13 5	50 0 0	do.
46 2 16	48 15 0	52 17 3	39 0 0	do.
79 0 34	40 15 0	44 2 6	34 11 11	do.
43 1 34	25 6 0	30 16 0	27 13 6	do.
148 0 27	50 10 0	78 10 0	63 12 6	do.
27 3 6	16 15 0	19 17 3	14 19 3	do.
40 0 6	14 2 0	19 10 0	14 4 3	do.
41 1 21	15 10 0	16 17 6	12 12 7	do.
44 0 35	40 5 0	51 17 6	40 0 0	
8 1 04	4 15 0	5 0 0	3 15 0	
29 1 0	20 15 0	24 0 0	17 10 0	
79 0 8	19 0 0	20 0 0	12 5 0	
8 0 7	12 0 0	20 0 0	13 10 0	
9 1 7	19 0 0	14 10 0	20 10 0	
6 3 32	9 15 0	16 10 0	9 17 6	
30 1 26	24 0 0	28 0 0	27 10 0	

Name of Assistant Commissioners by whom Cases were decided.	No.	Name of Tenant.	Name of Landlord.
Assistant Commissioners:—			
L. DOYLE (Legal.)	3560	Mary Sweeny, —	Daniel Gannon, —
J. J. OULKE.	3561	Barry Murphy, —	Richard T. Eyre, —
M. KELLY.	3562	John Barry Murphy, —	do. —
	3563	Michael Keane and anor.,	do. —
	3564	Jeremiah Lynch & anor.,	Francis G. Hewlson an
	3565	Jeremiah Ahern, senior,	Lieut.-Col. W. St. L. i well.
	3566	Ellen Sullivan, —	Rev. prop. T. Bennrich,
	3567	Mary Hennessy, Limited	do. —

CORK—continued.

Area of Holding.	Poor Law Valuation.	Former Rent.	Judicial Rent.	Observations.
A. R. P.	£ s. d.	£ s. d.	£ s. d.	
70 1 23	46 10 0	50 0 0	45 0 0	
43 3 11	33 5 0	43 5 1	34 13 5	
110 0 0	50 0 0	78 15 9	70 0 0	
43 3 0	35 15 0	54 13 0	35 0 0	
8 0 0	6 15 0	13 0 0	3 0 0	
68 1 19	17 15 0	23 6 0	14 10 0	
15 0 0	13 10 0	31 0 0	11 7 6	
22 2 20	14 0 0	13 10 0	10 8 6	
61 0 0	18 5 0	28 0 0	18 10 0	
9 8 20	6 0 0	10 0 0	3 15 0	
83 0 10	13 10 0	17 18 8	11 15 0	
60 2 11	20 5 0	33 6 0	24 17 6	
16 2 24	33 0 0	40 15 0	33 5 0	
26 0 19	17 15 0	31 0 0	33 13 4	
10 0 0	3 5 0	6 0 0	5 17 6	
17 1 0	11 0 0	17 0 0	13 0 0	
15 1 0	6 5 0	13 0 0	9 17 3	
24 3 35	11 10 0	19 0 6	13 0 0	
51 0 1	13 5 0	29 7 6	26 10 0	
70 5 14	24 10 0	39 13 10	33 8 0	
115 1 23	46 10 0	65 0 0	46 0 0	
14 0 34	31 15 0	42 7 8	28 10 0	Right of grazing on Kilno Mountain.
53 3 13	19 13 0	25 0 0	18 10 0	
19 0 37	13 5 0	20 15 3	14 10 0	
154 1 9	65 0 0	100 0 0	50 0 0	Right of grazing 30 on Lops Caherdowney Mountain.
79 8 2	14 10 0	20 0 0	33 10 0	Right of grazing 34 colleps, mountain.
101 0 0	67 10 0	120 1 2	53 10 0	

IRISH LAND COMMISSION.

COUNTY OF

Name of Assistant Commissioners by whom Cases were decided.	No.	Name of Tenant.	Name of Landlord.	Townland.
Assignee Consolidations—				
L. Doyle (Legal).	3803	Mary Kellahan, —	William F. Leader, —	Oakerbottagh, —
G. R. Bayly.	1208	Denis Twomey, —	Mrs. Kate Reardon, —	Knockmahon, —
R. W. Chalmers.	3804	Kate Kiely, —	Lieut.-Colonel Edward Nash,	Ballydaly,
	5304	Denis Maloney, —	do. — —	do. —
	5806	Patrick Carna, —	do. — —	do. —
	1507	Cornelius Harnett, —	Myles R. Burke and another,	Derrigh, —
	1508	James Sullivan, —	Dr. John Leader, —	Keale, —
	3809	Cornelius Murphy and another, sentd. in name of Mary Murphy.	Sir James L. Cotter and anor.	Garryguyne, —
	4800	Daniel O'Brien, —	do. — —	do. —
	3801	Cornelius Murphy, —	do. — —	do. —
	9407	Jeremiah Batlihy, —	do. — —	do. —
	3802	James Driscoll, —	James Creagh and another, —	Knockmahon, —
	8504	James Curran, —	do. — —	Healing, —
	4808	Patrick Scully and anot.,	James Morkery and another,	Killeenleen, —
	3808	Mary Scully, —	do. — —	do. —
	3807	John Ambrose, —	Charles J. Bagrun, —	Monkeroughan, —
	5408	Timothy Buckley, Trustee of R. Riordan and others.	Very Rev. Sowers Payne, —	Kilgobnet, —
	3809	Patrick Kelleher, Admor. of Jas. Kelleher, decd.	Henry G. Warren, —	Coherguguan, —
	3810	John Murphy, —	Harriett Organ and others, —	Coolabawne, —
	3611	Timothy Corcoran, —	do. — —	do. —
	3613	Patrick Corcoran, —	do. — —	do. —
	3613	John Hickey, —	Michael R. Crumb, —	Eaglans, —
	3514	Denis Duggan, —	do. — —	do. —
	3615	James Maloney, —	Lieut.-Colonel Edward Nash,	Ballydaly, —
				Total, —

CORK—*continued.*

Area of Holding.	Poor Law Valuation.	Former Rent.	Judicial Rent.	Observations.
a. r. p.	£ s. d.	£ s. d.	£ s. d.	
114 0 0	21 0 0	55 0 0	16 10 0	
79 3 14	71 10 0	61 0 0	25 10 0	
64 2 13	18 5 0	45 0 0	21 0 0	
11 6 1	7 15 0	15 0 0	7 10 0	
171 1 25	40 10 0	64 0 0	43 10 0	
10 1 18	14 15 0	30 0 0	32 10 0	
43 2 1	21 15 0	30 0 0	23 0 0	
120 0 0	17 0 0	30 0 0	20 0 0	
118 0 0	15 0 0	20 0 0	17 0 0	
29 0 0	3 10 0	8 17 0	4 4 0	
64 2 0	21 15 0	24 0 0	14 0 0	
91 0 0	1 14 0	5 17 0	6 10 0	
13 0 0	1 13 0	4 4 2	2 13 0	
41 1 0	23 0 6	51 0 0	19 5 3	
14 1 6	15 10 0	27 0 0	10 10 0	
97 0 0	21 16 0	65 10 0	50 0 0	By consent.
61 1 12	27 0 0	39 10 0	96 0 0	
23 0 6	18 10 0	22 10 0	20 0 0	
44 3 65	15 5 0	17 1 6	17 0 0	
42 2 15	17 6 0	22 0 0	16 0 0	
48 1 9	13 10 0	15 0 0	15 0 0	
14 0 0	17 6 0	19 6 10	16 0 0	
27 3 01	17 0 0	20 4 8	17 0 0	
29 1 19	9 19 0	15 0 0	6 10 0	
5,670 0 23	2,775 1 0	3,875 2 8	2,700 11 6	

LIMERICK.

Name of Assistant Commissioners by whom Cases were decided.	No.	Name of Tenant.	Name of Landlord.
Assistant Commissioners—			
J. R. Green, a.a. (Legal). H. G. Gerrard. W. H. Brereton.	1454	John Dalton, —	John Morgan, —
	1455	Allen Enright and anor.,	do. —
	1456	Cornelius O'Brien, ...	Lord Muskerry, ...
	1457	Michael O'Shaughnessy,	Miss Frances Bryan and
	1458	Catherine Hayes & anor.,	do. —
	1459	Patrick Sheehan, ...	do. —
	1460	Thomas Linane, —	Emma Aikinson, ...
	1461	Thomas O'Shaughnessy,	do. —
	1462	John Shaughnessy, —	do. —
	1463	Michael Hynes, ...	do. —
	1464	Patrick Hynes, ...	do. —
	1465	Edward Oxmann, —	John B. Blanquebamsi
	1466	Bridget Walsh, ...	do. —
	1467	Michael Galry, —	do. —
	1468	Mary Guinan and anor.,	do. —
	1469	John Shaughnessy and another,	do. —
	1470	Edward White, —	Thomas McO. Windle,
	1471	Thomas Walham, ..	do. —
	1472	James Pennell, —	do. —
	1473	William Pennell & anor.,	do. —

TABLE OF JUDICIAL RENTS

LIMERICK—*continued.*

Extent of Holdings. Acres.	Poor Law Valuation.	Former Rent.	Judicial Rent.	Observations
A. R. P.	£ s. d.	£ s. d.	£ s. d.	
63 1 28	7 10 0	80 0 8	8 0 0	
2 1 30	—	8 0 0	1 16 0	
18 0 83	34 0 0	44 0 0	23 10 0	
63 3 19	28 19 0	37 11 4	32 0 0	
15 3 4	33 0 8	42 8 0	38 8 0	
3 1 23	6 6 0	6 0 0	4 10 0	By agreement.
21 1 0	36 10 0	45 0 0	28 0 0	do.
85 3 23	17 5 0	28 0 0	19 0 0	do.
50 0 0	6 10 0	17 0 0	10 0 0	do.
37 1 83	13 15 0	21 6 8	16 0 0	do.
13 3 13	6 6 0	6 11 4	8 0 0	do.
30 3 6	unascertained,	14 10 0	11 0 0	do.
38 0 0	36 0 0	21 10 0	26 10 0	do.
13 1 8	7 8 0	10 10 0	7 10 0	do.
11 1 16	6 0 0	7 4 0	8 0 0	do.
63 0 0	unascertained,	20 10 0	17 0 0	do.
17 8 37	1 10 0	10 0 0	8 0 0	
21 3 10	1 0 0	8 0 0	6 0 0	
13 1 30	1 0 0	6 4 8	4 8 0	
13 3 80	0 6 0	13 10 0	7 10 0	
65 1 6	34 10 0	80 0 0	40 0 0	
50 1 83	34 15 0	60 0 0	61 10 0	
37 3 18	16 10 0	20 0 0	20 0 0	
13 0 80	0 16 0	8 10 0	8 0 0	
10 1 15	0 15 0	3 0 0	2 8 0	
28 3 14	0 13 0	3 10 0	8 10 0	
65 3 14	87 0 0	87 0 0	28 8 0	
58 1 17	34 0 0	36 0 6	70 0 0	
81 0 13	60 0 8	35 0 0	62 10 0	
81 0 8	11 6 0	10 0 0	16 0 0	
54 1 88	48 0 0	68 17 8	53 0 0	
63 0 88	31 15 0	60 0 0	31 0 0	
41 0 38	26 0 0	30 14 7	25 0 0	
129 0 17	107 0 0	113 0 0	105 0 0	
171 1 18	167 10 0	174 0 0	323 8 0	

Names of Assistant Commissioners by whom Cases were decided.	No.	Name of Tenant.	Name of Landlord.
Assistant Commissioners—			
J. S. Gunn, q.c. (Legal),	1479	James Hogan, ...	Le Marchant Dells
Jt. G. Gummy.	1480	Patrick Murvey, ...	La Marchant Dells Ba
W. M. Brownrig.	1481	Do, — ...	do. —
	1482	James O'Connor, ...	do. —
	1483	Catherine Malloy, ...	do. —
	1484	Maria T. Colbert, ...	do. ...o
	1485	James Danaher, —	do. ..o
	1486	James Meade, ...	do. ...
	1487	David McDonnell (Thomas)	do. —
	1488	David McDonnell and another.	do. —
	1489	Do, ... —	do. —
	1490	John Hawkins ...	do.

LIMERICK—continued.

Area of Holding. Statute.	Poor Law Valuation.	Former Rent.	Judicial Rent.	Observations.	Value of Tenancy.
A. R. P.	£ s. d.	£ s. d.	£ s. d.		£ s. d.
43 0 5	28 10 0	66 5 9	47 0 0		
66 1 0	25 0 0	60 0 0	40 0 0		
163 0 0	203 0 0	315 17 5	246 0 0		
41 3 36	81 5 0	34 13 1	30 0 0		
138 3 33	148 14 0	134 13 0	144 0 0		
68 0 33	44 10 0	66 16 3	43 0 0		
37 0 33	27 15 0	48 14 6	40 0 0		
140 1 0	175 0 0	220 5 4	175 0 0		
16 0 6	16 10 0	34 16 6	14 10 0		
71 3 34	53 0 0	102 8 4	75 0 0		
63 3 8	53 0 0	145 4 7	101 0 0		
144 1 4	151 0 0	193 5 9	140 0 0		
2,637 0 13	1,953 0 0	3,047 17 6	2,143 16 0		

TIPPERARY.

61 3 13	84 0 0	33 10 0	24 0 0	By consent.	
13 1 5	10 10 0	16 0 0	12 0 0		
6 0 14	6 15 0	10 0 0	8 0 0		
110 3 22	90 4 0	90 0 0	65 0 0		
43 3 4	41 0 0	77 0 0	60 0 0		
53 1 7	38 0 0	33 10 0	24 0 0		
53 0 5	28 15 0	31 0 0	34 0 0		
317 1 30	309 5 0	300 16 3	315 0 0		
46 3 14	33 0 0	40 12 2	37 0 0		
137 3 1	68 0 0	100 0 0	77 0 0		
141 0 31	85 0 0	90 14 0	60 0 0		
56 3 23½	90 6 0	50 0 0	38 0 0		
141 0 36	60 0 0	60 0 0	64 0 0		
243 0 6	115 8 0	114 18 8	85 0 0		
28 3 13	22 16 0	23 1 1	22 1 1		

Printed image digitised by the University of Southampton Library Digitisation Unit

Name of Assistant Commissioner by whom Case was decided	No.	Name of Tenant	Name of Landlord
Assistant Commissioners—			
J. H. Knox (Legal).	1148	James Buckett,	John Fennelly,
F. M. Caswell.	1149	Richard Kee,	Mrs. Martha Cornwall
S. G. Pezz.	1150	John Kavanagh,	Henry J. Lloyd,
	1151	Do.,	do.
	1152	John Ryan (Martin),	Miss Grace Grehan,
	1153	Do.,	do.
	1154	James Fogarty,	do.
J. H. Knox (Legal).	1155	James Quaid,	William Ryan, assist. 1 of G. A. Ryan.
L. Corbett.	1156	Body Carmody,	George Bolton,
B. M. French.	1157	Daniel Boland,	do.
	1158	John F. Hayes,	G. R. Smithwick,
	1159	Matilda Byrne,	Charles S. Grehan,
	1160	William Finnistry,	Captain R. Heard,
	1161	Bridget Mahon,	Henry B. S. Merrigan
	1162	Mary Stapleton, Bridget, et Richard Stapleton, her guardian,	do.
	1163	William Lehane,	W. E. Marshall,
	1164	Dr. Patrick M. Cleary, assnd. in name of Richd. M. Cleary,	William H. Head, in name of William H.
	1165	Michael Cleary,	Miss Marie O'Brien &c.
	1166	Delton Garrett,	Mrs. Olivia Rowallan
	1167	Patrick Murphy,	Miss Julia Barrington &c.
	1168	Edward Donohoe,	John K. Delaney,
	1169	Michael Mahet,	George L. Madlin,
	1170	Dan Mahet,	do.
	1171	Margaret Costigan,	do.
	1172	Peter Maher,	do.
	1173	Margaret Clancy,	John Finn,

TIPPERARY—*continued.*

Extent of Holding, Statute	Poor Law Valuation	Former Rents	Judicial Rent
A. R. P.	£ s. d.	£ s. d.	£ s. d.
24 1 8	11 15 0	14 4 9	11 10 0
148 6 8	185 10 0	204 13 4	160 0 0
31 1 31	unascertained,	33 13 3	29 0 0
16 2 16	do.	23 7 11	16 0 0
43 0 16	14 10 0	27 6 0	20 0 0
13 0 17	6 0 0	8 10 0	6 18 0
13 2 20	9 0 0	16 14 0	10 10 0
61 1 57	81 10 0	81 15 4	22 6 0
46 0 0	3 15 0	4 0 0	3 6 0
73 1 21	47 15 0	70 0 0	48 17 0
12 0 10	11 0 0	20 3 2	17 15 0
523 1 20	808 0 0	909 4 8	193 3 3
134 0 12	36 0 0	40 0 0	34 12 0
10 3 30	9 0 0	18 0 0	9 28 0
35 1 0	16 6 0	20 0 0	16 1 0
65 1 4	34 15 0	52 0 0	49 18 0
61 1 62	37 10 0	50 6 0	62 3 0
39 2 10	40 6 0	50 0 0	20 0 0
144 3 30	57 0 0	70 0 0	65 7 0
72 0 24	43 15 0	65 13 9	40 16 0
12 1 83	11 0 0	16 10 0	18 10 0
20 2 0½	19 10 0	16 1 7	16 1 7
30 3 50	6 15 0	13 13 10	10 19 0
12 0 8	18 0 0	17 17 0	17 17 0
19 0 0½	16 0 0	11 19 0	10 19 0
2 3 31	unascertained,	3 10 0	2 3 4
16 0 29	6 10 0	5 14 4	4 13 6
16 1 4	4 5 0	5 6 0	6 16 6
59 6 83	21 15 0	20 5 1	84 10 0
8 3 16	9 10 0	8 13 3	8 6 0
24 0 31	11 10 0	16 13 6	13 7 0

Name of Arbitrators Nominated by whom Case was notified	No.	Name of Tenant	Name of Landlord	Townland
Assistant Commissioners— J. R. Brown, &c. (Legal). J. Hamorok, J. J. O'Sexparameter.	267	James Eagle,	Miss M. Gordon,	Knockfuan,
	268	Joseph Nugent,	Duke of Saint Albans,	Barravakeen,
	269	Thomas Power,	do.	Oldkicheen,
	270	Edward Harrahan,	do.	do.
	271	Michael Dolan,	Lord Ashtown,	Carraghtuigum,
	272	William Devine,	do.	Carraghtuoloy,
	273	William Corrigan,	do.	do.
	274	Patrick Mulligan,	do.	do.
	275	John Nugent,	do.	Toorragh,
	276	Richard Moran,	do.	Kilattigaan,
	277	William Moran,	do.	do.
	278	John Ormond,	do.	Glisho,
	279	Do.,	do.	Quirraghanabbog,
	280	James Gordon,	do.	Grolgraganaig,
	281	Patrick Gordon, Tail Assignor of Thomas Gordon,	do.	do.
	282	Mary Gordon, Tail Assignor of John Gordon,	do.	do.
	283	James Phelan,	do.	do.
	284	Patrick Power,	do.	do.
	285	Alice Flynn, Rep. of Patrick Flynn,	do.	Crossglanakin,
	286	Catherine Moran,	do.	do.
	287	Thomas Flynn,	do.	do.
	288	Thomas Kilfoy,	do.	do.
	289	Thomas Dacy (John),	do.	Dunepark and Coolroe,
	290	Patrick Naughton, Tail Assignor of Michael Naughton,	do.	do.
	291	Michael Dacey,	do.	Liwingnirk,
	292	William Long, &c., Assignor of Thomas Dacy,	do.	do.
	293	Thomas Reader,	do.	Crossglanak and do.
	294	John Morris,	do.	do.
	295	John Phelan,	do.	Ballygungarosa,
	296	Margaret Burgin,	do.	do.
	297	James Ormond,	do.	Claghlena,
	298	James Kelleher,	do.	Tooraluigh,
				Total,

WATERFORD.

Extent of Holding Acreage	Poor Law Valuation	Former Rent	Judicial Rent	Observations
A. R. P.	£ s. d.	£ s. d.	£ s. d.	
7 1 3	11 10 0	12 0 0	9 0 0	
543 0 11	123 0 0	141 3 9	146 0 0	
213 5 11	76 10 0	110 0 0	78 10 0	
713 5 10	69 0 0	110 0 0	70 0 0	
62 1 20	37 10 0	47 0 0	30 0 0	
116 5 0	60 12 0	75 12 6	47 5 9	
104 3 7	26 10 0	60 0 0	34 0 0	
56 0 9	9 6 0	20 0 0	10 10 0	
53 0 22	25 17 0	56 0 0	33 15 0	
50 0 0	10 0 0	23 0 0	16 0 0	
62 0 11	24 0 0	44 0 0	30 10 0	
66 3 22	48 0 0	75 0 0	60 0 0	
111 3 34	41 0 0	67 0 0	49 10 0	
79 2 6	18 15 0	54 0 0	23 10 0	
78 2 9	16 10 0	23 0 0	23 0 0	
79 3 5	17 10 0	29 0 0	34 0 0	
189 1 23	37 10 0	65 0 0	41 0 0	
65 1 07	14 0 0	29 0 0	22 0 0	
122 1 23	41 0 0	82 0 0	47 5 0	
96 0 10	65 0 0	90 0 0	44 15 0	
3 3 30	63 0 0	91 0 0	53 0 0	
61 1 0	32 0 0	74 0 0	44 10 0	
23 0 9	15 17 0	21 0 0	16 0 0	
41 3 17	19 0 0	28 10 0	21 0 0	
31 1 10	37 0 0	50 0 0	33 0 0	
44 3 11	25 11 0	61 0 0	23 0 0	
62 1 0	23 5 0	63 10 0	34 0 0	

CIVIL BILL

PROVINCE OF

COUNTY OF

County Court Judge.	No.	Name of Tenant.	Name of Landlord.	Townland.
W. H. Edens, q.c.	5	Mons Jackson & ors.,	Charles Stanley,	Ballinasy,

COUNTY OF

County Court Judge	No.	Name of Tenant	Name of Landlord	Townland
Charles Watson, q.c.	209	Patrick Boylan,	Catherine Rashuck,	Derryfinan Lowe, and another.
	210	Benjamin Cunning	Henry & Singleton,	Drumlan,
	211	Joseph Reilly,	do.	do.
	212	James Sheridan,	do.	do.
	213	Phillip Duffy,	Rev. Robert Quinty,	Drumlan,
				Total,

PROVINCE OF

COUNTY OF

County Court Judge	No.	Name of Tenant	Name of Landlord	Townland
Frederick B. Falkiner, q.c.	1	William McGuинas,	Minns Hopkinson,	Hill of the Grange,

Digitized or produced by the University Association of Library Institute of Oregon 1907

COURTS.

ULSTER.

ARMAGH.

Area of Holding. Acres.	Poor Law Valuation.	Former Rent.	Judicial Rent.	Observations.
£ s. d.	£ s. d.	£ s. d.	£ s. d.	
33 0 19	undetermined,	41 15 0	30 0 0	

CAVAN.

93 0 8	71 10 0	94 19 10	64 8 0	
5 1 0	2 10 0	3 15 6	1 15 0	
7 0 0	8 18 0	8 17 10	4 0 0	
19 1 25	11 8 0	13 1 6	9 18 0	
85 0 0	83 0 0	30 0 0	21 0 0	
139 9 33	116 0 0	146 14 3	100 18 6	

LEINSTER.

DUBLIN.

CIVIL BILL COURTS.

County Court Judge.	No.	Name of Tenant.	Name of Landlord.	Townland.
W. F. Darley, q.c.	23	John Brownlow, ...	Thomas J. De Burgh, ...	Naas, West, ...
	14	Mary Quinn, ...	Sir Arthur P. F. Aylmer, Bt.,	Lickinpora, ...
				Total. ...

Gerald Fitzgerald,	168	Richard Smith, ...	Miss Armstrong, ...	Milltown, ...
	107	Stephen Kelly, ...	W. R. Supple, ...	Dunshaughlin, ...
				Total. ...

PROVINCE OF

MEATH.

64	0	9	31	0
13	3	11	4	0
47	9	90	58	0

MUNSTER.

KERRY.

COUNTY OF

No.	Name of Tenant	Name of Landlord	Townland
135	John Burns,	William O. Sanders,	Inchenagog,
136	James Burrell,	do.	do.
137	Michael Lee,	do.	do.
138	Timothy Dowding,	do.	Francis, West,
139	Mary O'Connor,	do.	Kilcummin, East,
140	Deborah Fitzgerald,	John McGillicuddy,	Ballynbeen,
141	Thomas Foley,	do.	do.
142	John Clifford,	do.	Kilbrugh,
143	John Connor,	do.	do.
144	Mary Griffin,	do.	do.
145	John Brien,	Henry A. Herbert,	Dromcummer,
146	Edan Doraghtie,	The O'Donoghue,	do.
147	Catherine Jeffcott, Rep. of Robert Jeffcott	Sir John F. Godfrey, Bart.,	Ballymenican and district,
148	Eugene Courtenay,	Daniel O'B Courtenay,	Curismullin,
			Total,

Rent fixed upon the Reports of Valuers appointed by the Irish

PROVINCE OF

COUNTY OF

KERRY—continued.

Extent of Holding. Area.	Poor Law Valuation.	Former Rent.	Judicial Rent.	Observations.	Term of Tenancy.
A. R. P.	£ s. d.	£ s. d.	£ s. d.		£ d.
43 3 20	0 3 6	18 0 6	6 6 0		
68 3 36	5 10 2	10 9 0	5 10 0		
68 0 13	0 8 0	11 0 0	5 14 9		
73 2 10	8 10 0	14 8 0	10 0 0		
138 1 9	36 5 0	66 8 0	68 10 0		
114 2 22	27 5 0	44 10 0	34 0 0		
99 0 0	8 10 0	14 0 0	11 10 0		
3 0 0	0 19 6	6 0 0	4 17 6		
52 3 14	10 12 0	18 0 0	12 17 6	With right of grazing on mountain.
58 1 44	5 5 0	12 0 0	9 17 6	With right of grazing eight couples on mountain.
59 2 5	14 10 0	32 10 0	30 0 0	With right of grazing ½ of hills. On bog, undivided.
158 0 0	16 10 0	34 0 0	31 0 0	
8 3 37	7 0 0	15 0 0	10 0 0	
28 4 34	9 0 6	34 0 6	14 8 0	
1,480 3 35	379 1 0	641 16 10	635 1 9	

Land Commission on the Joint Application of Landlord and Tenant

LEINSTER.

DUBLIN: Printed for Her Majesty's Stationery Office,
By ALEX. THOM & Co. (Limited), 87, 88, & 89, Abbey-street
The Queen's Printing Office

www.ingramcontent.com/pod-product-compliance
Lightning Source LLC
Chambersburg PA
CBHW030610270326
41927CB00007B/1105

* 9 7 8 3 7 4 2 8 0 0 2 2 0 *